Education in the Republic of South Sudan

STATUS AND CHALLENGES
FOR A NEW SYSTEM

AFRICA HUMAN
DEVELOPMENT SERIES

Education in the Republic of South Sudan

STATUS AND CHALLENGES
FOR A NEW SYSTEM

AFRICA HUMAN
DEVELOPMENT SERIES

THE WORLD BANK
Washington, D.C.

Contents

TABLES

Foreword

The January 2011 referendum—in which an overwhelming majority of the people of South Sudan voted for independence—was a major rallying point in the establishment of a new relationship between the state and the people. As with any such relationship, there are responsibilities and expectations. In the brand new country of the Republic of South Sudan, one of the most important areas where government and citizens will converge closely is education.

This Education Status Report (ESR),[1] prepared at the request of the Government of South Sudan (GoSS), provides a comprehensive snapshot of an education sector that is emerging from a long period of civil strife. It confirms the strong appetite among the people for education; in turn, more educated citizens are needed to provide the bedrock of the new country and its prospects. The purpose of this report is to enhance the knowledge base for policy development in the education sector and, more broadly, create a platform for engaging a diverse audience in dialogue on education policies in the new country. The ultimate aim is to help develop a shared vision for the future of the education system among government, citizens, and partners in Africa's newest nation.

The report clearly shows that the education system in South Sudan faces all the challenges of a new nation that is making a visible effort to catch up quickly from a very low base by rapidly increasing student enrollment. These challenges include a concentration of students in the early grades; a high proportion of overage students, repetition, and dropout; and weak levels of student learning. With an estimated one million out-of-school children and a primary school completion rate of only 26 percent, South Sudan needs to expand the capacity of the education system, but in an increasingly selective and strategic manner—the out-of-school children increasingly have a particular profile: poor, rural, female, and overage. Further, the report indicates that South Sudan is beginning to feel the effects of its success at increasing enrollment at the primary level with growing demand for secondary and higher education.

A key finding of the report is that resources made available to the education sector could be allocated and deployed more efficiently. Although significant progress has been made toward establishing a functioning payroll system for teachers and other education staff in the states, staff are not distributed equally across schools in proportion to enrollment. South Sudan will need more teachers and more pedagogical inputs, but these must be better managed. The report also highlights the low overall quality of education, and emphasizes that quality of education and accountability of the education sector should become central considerations early on in the development of the education system.

Finally, the report emphasizes the importance of South Sudan's unique Alternative Education System (AES), which will continue to play a central part in the education system for years to come. The majority of youth and adults in the country today may never benefit from formal basic education, but their learning needs must be met if South Sudan is to build a solid state and society. The AES is currently offering accelerated learning programs to more than 200,000 youth and adults and holds significant promise.

The report was prepared when the education system was undergoing rapid change. Since April 2005, when the Joint Assessment Mission for Sudan prepared a framework that described the capacity building necessary in South Sudan to provide adequate services and improve progress toward the Millennium Development Goals, the GoSS has made remarkable progress in building institutions and improving service delivery, including in education. When we received the government's request for assistance with the preparation of this report, an Education Management Information System (EMIS) had already been set up and a population census had just been launched, so some of the information needed for system diagnostics was starting to become available. Data analyzed in this report have been collected and triangulated from various sources, including the population data from the 2008 census, the payroll database for the education sector for 2009, and the first National Baseline Household Survey of 2009.

This report has been prepared with funding from the Education Program Development Fund, a multi-donor trust fund established within the framework of the Education For All Fast Track Initiative (now Global Partnership for Education) to help low-income countries accelerate progress toward universal primary completion. The ESR was prepared with significant collaboration with the Ministry of Education and development partners. It currently serves as a key input to the development of a comprehensive education sector strategy.

Besides contributing to ongoing discussions on education between the government and its development partners, the report is a comprehensive resource for all who are interested in education in the Republic of South Sudan. Furthermore, it has contributed to the development of national capacity for education sector analysis. Our hope is that these contributions will help the Republic of South Sudan develop the well-educated citizenry that is necessary for all nations in the twenty-first century.

Ritva Reinikka
Director
Human Development Department
Africa Region
The World Bank

NOTE

1. The ESR is part of a series of Education Country Status Reports prepared for more than 30 countries in the Africa Region since around 2000. The ESR follows a structure developed by the World Bank, which allows easy comparisons between countries. Education Country Status Reports for other countries can be accessed at www.worldbank.org/afr/education.

Acknowledgments

This report benefited from financial support from the Global Partnership for Education's (GPE's)[1] Education Program Development Fund (EPDF) and from the Multi-Donor Trust Fund for Southern Sudan.

The report was prepared jointly by a national team and a World Bank team. The national team was led by Mr. Hakim Dabi, Deputy Director of Data and Statistics, Government of the Republic of South Sudan (GoRSS) Ministry of Education (MoE), and included other staff from the MoE as well as from the state ministries of education: Esther Akumu, John Lujang, Mangbi Atanasio, Duku Azaria, Odur Nelson, Mading Manyok, Anthony Lopirto, Peter Oyech Martin, Martin Manyang, Mario Alex, Manoah Machile Milla, Gideon Kuc, and Sami Musuku. Shadrak Chol, Director General of MoE, provided overall guidance to the Education Status Report (ESR) team.

The Service Delivery Study was carried out by Juba University and the Southern Sudan Centre for Census, Statistics and Evaluation (SSCCSE) in close collaboration with the World Bank team. The team from Juba University that braved the difficult and often unsafe terrains in the four states surveyed was led by Lino Gwaki and included Joseph Badys, Peter Diaak, Victor Fifa, Otim Gama, Dominic Jada, James Koma, David Mawa, and Sandra Mekele. Data entry was performed by the SSCCSE.

The World Bank team consisted of Ramahatra Rakotomalala (Task Team Leader), Prema Clarke, Kirsten Majgaard, and Koffi Segniagbeto. Ryoko Tomita Wilcox assisted the team in completing the report. Michel Welmond, the World Bank Education Cluster Leader for the Republic of South Sudan, provided overall guidance to the team. Ian Bannon (Country Director) and Peter Materu (Sector Manager) ensured management oversight. Chris Kenyi and Getahun Gebru, the World Bank's education team in Juba, facilitated the team's interaction with government and donor representatives in country. Joyce Gamba and Rosario Aristorenas provided administrative support.

The team would like to acknowledge the contribution of a number of other people to the Education Status Report: the director generals of the state ministries of education, most of whom interacted with the team during workshops in Juba or during visits to the states; members of the Education Management Information System (EMIS) Unit, in particular Fahim Akbar, Lene Leonhardsen, Bosun Jang, and Moses Olaki; George Monga and Martin Luther Luduku from MoE; Martin Abucha and other staff from the National Bureau of Statistics; Grace Akukwe from the Academy for Educational Development (AED) Technical Assistance Program for the Republic of South Sudan; Charles Goldsmith and Simon Lewis from Booz & Company; Charles Nabongo from the United Nations Children's Fund (UNICEF); and representatives from all development partners who shared their insights or interacted with the team in workshops or other meetings.

At the concept note stage, the report benefited from comments from Laurence Clarke, Peter Buckland, Sanjeev Ahluwalia, Peter Darvas, and Linda English. The United States Agency for International Development (USAID) also provided valuable comments at the concept stage. During preparation, Bill Battaile and Deepa Sankar provided expert advice. Elizabeth Ninan, Shwetlana Sabarwal, and Nathalie Lahire provided comments to an initial draft. Peer reviewers were Lianqin Wang, Joel Reyes, Flora Kelmendi, and Luis Crouch. All contributions are gratefully acknowledged.

NOTE

1. The GPE was formerly known as the Education For All (EFA) Fast Track Initiative (FTI). Web site: www.globalpartnership.org.

Abbreviations

AED	Academy for Educational Development
AES	Alternative Education System
ALP	Accelerated Learning Programme
CEC	Cluster Education Center
CGS	Community-based Girls' Schools
CPA	Comprehensive Peace Agreement
CR	Completion Rate
ECD	Early Childhood Development
EFA	Education For All
EMIS	Education Management Information System
EPDF	Education Program Development Fund
ESR	Education Status Report
FTI	Fast Track Initiative
FTTP	Fast Track Training Program
GDP	Gross Domestic Product
GER	Gross Enrollment Rate
GIR	Gross Intake Rate
GoNU	Government of National Unity
GoRSS	Government of the Republic of South Sudan
GPE	Global Partnership for Education
GPS	Global Positioning System
IDP	Internally Displaced Person
IEA	International Association for the Evaluation of Educational Achievement
IEC	Intensive English Course
IOM	International Organization for Migration
IRI	Interactive Radio Instruction

JAM	Joint Assessment Mission
LAY	Latest Available Year
MDG	Millennium Development Goal
MDTF	Multi-Donor Trust Fund
MENA	Middle East and North Africa
MoE	Ministry of Education
MoEST	Ministry of Education, Science and Technology (title of MoE until 2010)
MoGE	(Federal) Ministry of General Education
MoHEST	Ministry of Higher Education, Science and Technology
NBHS	National Baseline Household Survey
NGO	Nongovernmental Organization
PCR	Primary Completion Rate
PIRLS	Progress in International Reading Literacy Study
PSTC	Primary School Leaving Certificate
PTA	Parent-Teacher Association
PTR	Pupil-Teacher Ratio
R^2	Coefficient of Determination in Statistical Analysis
RALS	Rapid Assessment of Learning Spaces
RoSS	Republic of South Sudan
SBA	School-Based Assessment
SDG	Sudanese Pound
SDS	Service Delivery Study
SHHS	Sudan Household Health Survey
SMoE	State Ministry of Education
SPLM/A	Sudan People's Liberation Movement/Army
SSA	Sub-Saharan Africa
SSCCSE	Southern Sudan Centre for Census, Statistics and Evaluation (now the Republic of South Sudan National Bureau of Statistics)
TIMSS	Trends in International Mathematics and Science Study
TTI	Teacher Training Institute
UN	United Nations
UNICEF	United Nations Children's Fund
UPC	Universal Primary Completion
USAID	United States Agency for International Development
WDI	World Development Indicators

Executive Summary

With the signing of the Comprehensive Peace Agreement (CPA) in 2005 came the establishment of a new education system specifically for the Republic of South Sudan.[1] Before the CPA, the relatively few schools operating in South Sudan were not part of a coordinated education system. During the second civil war, for example, most schools were run by missionaries, communities, or nongovernmental organizations (NGOs). Schools differed widely on almost all counts: duration of the primary and secondary cycles; curriculum (Ethiopian, Kenyan, Sudanese, or Ugandan); language of instruction (English, Arabic); and mode of organization. Toward the end of the second civil war, the Sudan Peoples' Liberation Movement started organizing schools, often with demobilized soldiers as teachers (who received no formal pay). Since the signing of the CPA and implementation of its power- and wealth-sharing protocols, the education system is now under significant transformation. For the first time, a coordinated education system is being put in place supported by public resources to serve the entire population of South Sudan.

This Education Status Report (ESR), *Education in the Republic of South Sudan: Status and Challenges for a New System*, provides a diagnostic of the education system in South Sudan and sheds light on such questions as the following: Is everyone getting a chance at education? How much are students learning? What is the situation of schools and service delivery? What is the country investing in education and how is it using these resources? Are the resources well deployed and managed to ensure efficient functioning of the education system?

IS EVERYONE GETTING A CHANCE AT EDUCATION?

The education system in South Sudan has been in a "catch-up phase" of development over the past decade. School enrollments have risen spectacularly since around 2000. Primary school enrollments approximately doubled between 2000 and 2005 from 0.3 million to 0.7 million, and then again between 2005 and 2009 from 0.7 million to 1.4 million. As a result, the primary school gross enrollment rate (GER) increased from an estimated 21 percent in 2000 to 72 percent in 2009, an impressive feat by any measure that speaks to the commitment of the people of South Sudan to educating their children. Although data are less complete for secondary education, enrollments at this level have at least doubled since 2005. As a result of the expansion in enrollments, access to education has improved dramatically, although many children are still out of school. Currently, 60 percent of 13-year-olds report having attended formal schooling, up from 40 percent a decade ago.

The recent rapid growth after a long period of stagnation has resulted in a concentration of students in the early grades, a high proportion of overage students, repetition, and dropout. The schooling profile, based on data from the Education Management Information System (EMIS), shows that few students attend the upper primary grades, resulting in a primary completion rate that is still very low at only 26 percent for grade 6 and 8 percent for grade 8 (figure 1). Overage enrollment is a widespread feature of the education system: in primary schools, as many as 44 percent of students are five or more years overage for their grade. Further, many primary school students repeat grades. In grade 1 in particular, as many as 23 per-

Figure 1 Cross-Sectional Schooling Profile Based on EMIS, 2009

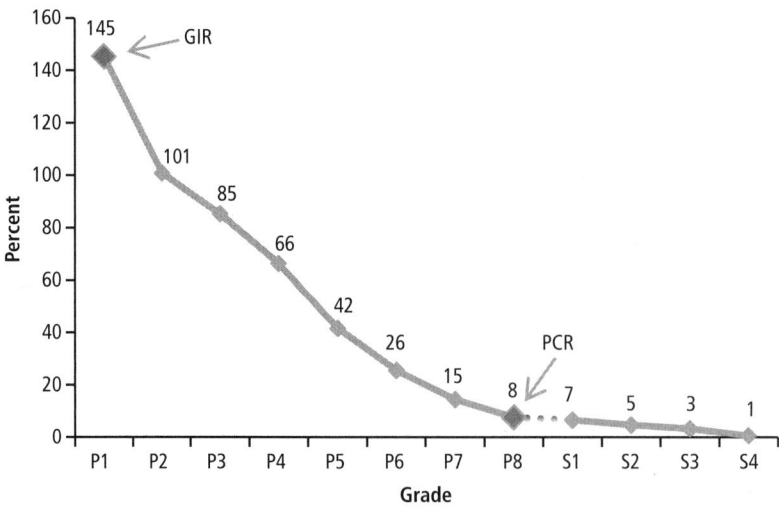

Source: Analysis of EMIS 2009 and population data.
Note: The data points of the schooling profiles are calculated as nonrepeaters divided by population of relevant age.

cent could be repeaters. Based on EMIS data, retention of students is fairly good until grade 4 (70 percent), but after grade 4, dropout is steep and only 18 percent of those who enrolled in grade 1 are still in school by grade 8. Although overage enrollment will be a feature of the system for the next several years, over time this is likely to self-correct as children start enrolling closer to the official age and the "multicohort" effect diminishes. Other aspects are more at risk of becoming permanent features of the education system, such as the high repetition and dropout rates.

With a primary completion rate (PCR) for the first six years of schooling of 26 percent, there is a very long road ahead to attaining universal primary completion (UPC). The PCR is a key indicator of progress toward UPC, a Millennium Development Goal (MDG). UPC usually refers to completion of a primary cycle of around six years, generally deemed necessary to provide children with basic skills, including lifelong literacy.

Furthermore, disparities in school participation rates are quite substantial in South Sudan. The widest disparities are associated with the urbanrural and rich-poor dimensions, but there are also strong gender disparities. Recent survey data indicate higher primary completion rates than EMIS data, but confirm wide disparities. Based on survey data, the chance of completing the eight-year primary cycle is currently 30 percent for boys but only 17 percent for girls. Regional disparities are also very wide as shown in figure 2, which divides the 10 states into three groups based on

Figure 2   Disparities in Primary School GER across States, 2009

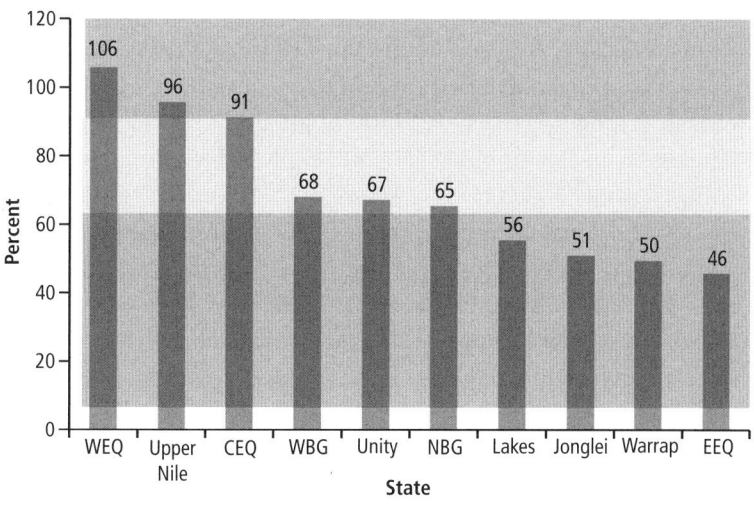

Source: Analysis of the 2009 National Baseline Household Survey (NBHS).
Note: CEQ = Central Equatoria; EEQ = Eastern Equatoria; NBG = Northern Bahr Ghazal; WBG = Western Bahr Ghazal; WEQ = Western Equatoria.

the primary school gross enrollment rate. The chance of completing the primary cycle averages 35 percent in the three "high enrollment" states shown but only 14 percent in the four "low enrollment" states. Although the gap between boys' and girls' enrollment still affects all levels of education, it has diminished greatly, resulting in a much smaller gender gap in the current generation of children than among adults. This shows that girls are among the main beneficiaries of the recent expansion in educational coverage. Gaps in school participation remain, however, and girls are also affected by higher repetition and dropout rates than boys.

The secondary and higher education subsectors are relatively small in South Sudan. Despite a rapid growth in secondary enrollments, the secondary school gross enrollment rate, at 6 percent, is still much lower than the average for Sub-Saharan Africa (SSA). Few schools actually operate with the official four-year secondary cycle, but rather run either three-year or six-year cycles. This shows that many schools still operate under a foreign curriculum, for example, following the Kenyan or Ugandan system. Repetition in secondary schools may be significantly higher than the 6 percent reported by EMIS. In 2009, higher education enrollments totaled 23,968, most of whom were enrolled at the Khartoum campuses of South Sudan's three public universities: Juba, Bahr El Ghazal, and Upper Nile University. Only about 6,500 students were enrolled in higher education at South Sudan campuses in 2009; 83 percent of these are enrolled in public institutions and 17 percent in one of five newly established private universities.

The Alternative Education System (AES) is the second largest part of the education system, with more than 200,000 students (equal to approximately 18 percent of the enrollment of primary school). It offers learning opportunities to children and adults who either have never attended formal education or have attended school but dropped out and are not likely to reenroll. It offers a variety of learning programs, including some targeted to active and demobilized Sudan People's Liberation Army (SPLA) and other security forces. Seven main components are currently being implemented, often in partnerships with other organizations and with the support of the development partners: Accelerated Learning Programmes (ALPs), Community-based Girls' Schools (CGS), Adult Education, Intensive English Course (IEC), Interactive Radio Instruction (IRI), Pastoralist Education, and Agro-forestry Education. ALPs account for more than 75 percent of reported AES enrollments.

South Sudan has an estimated 1 million out-of-school children, 925,000 of whom live in rural areas. Clearly, children in urban areas are much more likely to be enrolled in any level of education than rural children (figure 3). For this reason, and because most of the population live in

Figure 3 Youth Cohorts by Level of Schooling in Urban and Rural Areas, 2009

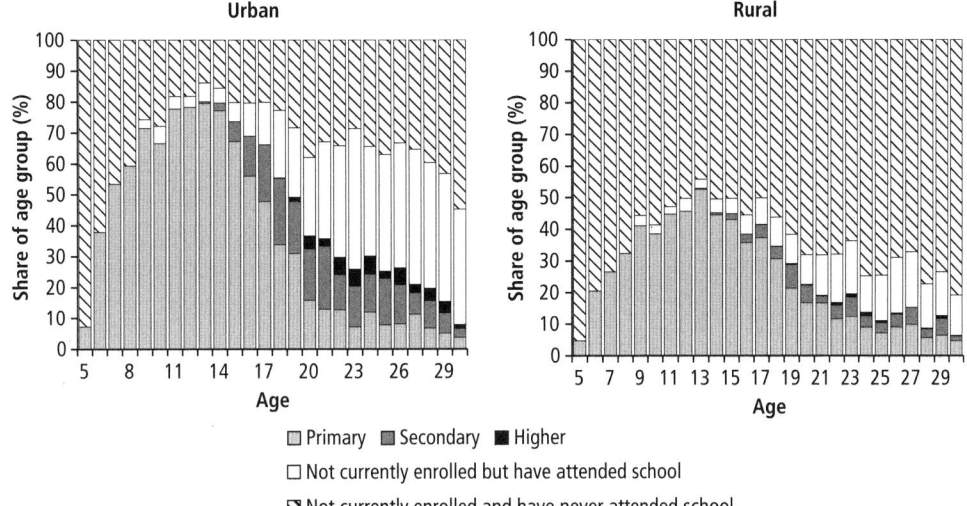

Source: Analysis of the 2009 NBHS.

rural areas, by far most out-of-school children—that is, children who should be in primary school but are not attending school—are rural: 27 percent are out of school in urban areas compared to 58 percent in rural areas, for a South Sudan average of 53 percent out of school. This translates into 1 million out-of-school children.

HOW MUCH ARE STUDENTS LEARNING?

A test of student learning of sixth-graders in a sample of mostly urban schools in four states finds weak levels of learning in both language and mathematics.[2] In language, students got 35 percent of test questions right, while in mathematics, students answered correctly 29 percent of the time. (To give an idea of the range, both tests were composed of multiple choice questions that each had four possible answers, so a randomly completed test questionnaire would give an average score of around 25 percent. Fourth-graders in Singaporean schools score around 80 percent in a similar test.) These results are no surprise, given the history of education in South Sudan and considering that many other low-income csountries in both SSA and other parts of the world are struggling to achieve acceptable levels of student learning. Comparing the South Sudan sample with results found in other developing countries that have used the same or similar tests, we find that the South Sudan school sample performed a little better than Benin, approximately on par with the Republic of Yemen, but not as good as the Republic of Sudan in mathematics. For the test in language, the situation is similar. The same test was also administered to 160 teachers across the four states. The mean score for teachers was 63 percent in mathematics and 62 percent in language.

WHAT IS THE SITUATION OF SCHOOLS AND SERVICE DELIVERY?

Primary schools tend to be overcrowded, class sizes are large, and schools rarely offer the complete primary cycle. Between 2002 and 2009, the average enrollment in a primary school doubled to 429 students, resulting in many overcrowded schools. In 2009, the average pupil-teacher ratio in primary schools was 52 when volunteer teachers are included and 81 excluding volunteers, and there were 129 pupils per classroom, on average. Most of the primary schools (75 percent) and some of the secondary schools (22 percent) do not have permanent structures, which leads to the loss of school working days. High average class sizes make instruction a challenge, and there is a severe shortage of textbooks in both primary and secondary schools. In primary schools, the average pupil-textbook ratio is 3:1 in both mathematics and English. Two-thirds of the students surveyed in the Service Delivery Study, a school survey carried out by Juba University and Southern Sudan Centre for Census, Statistics and Evaluation (SSCCSE), did not have paper to write on and one-fifth of the students did not have pens or other writing instruments; this limits opportunities for reinforcing what is taught. As many as 87 percent of primary schools do not offer students the complete eight-year primary cycle. Less than half of primary schools have grade 6 and only 13 percent of schools offered grade 8 in 2009. The high share of incomplete schools represents a principal constraint to attaining the MDG of universal primary completion (six years of schooling or more).

WHAT IS THE REPUBLIC OF SOUTH SUDAN INVESTING IN EDUCATION AND HOW IS IT USING THESE RESOURCES?

Due to a budgetary crisis, public education spending declined after its 2008 peak and is now lower than when the CPA was established. Since the school-age population is growing every year, this has led to a decline in public education spending per child (figure 4). The sector receives between 5 and 8 percent of total Government of the Republic of South Sudan (GoRSS) spending; a share that has remained more or less stable over the years. The primary cycle as a whole receives 55 percent of public recurrent education spending. *Thus, the budget allocation to the first six*

Figure 4 Trend in Spending Effort: Public Education Spending per Child (Ages 6–16), 2006–09

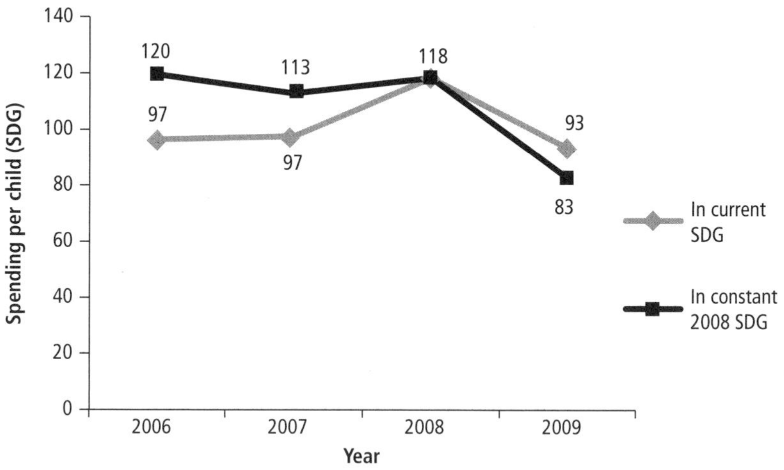

Source: Ministry of Finance and Economic Planning (MoFEP) budget books, 2007–10.
Note: Data for 2006–08 are actuals, for 2009 provisional.

years of primary education is approximately 45–50 percent, a level comparable to other countries in the region. Secondary education receives 18 percent and higher education 19 percent, when financing by the Government of National Unity (GoNU) is included.

Salaries constitute the largest spending component, on average, 77 percent of total GoRSS education spending. *There are about 51,000 education staff working in the 10 states; only 30,616 of these are on payroll, while some 20,000 are not.* Almost half of staff working in the schools are volunteers. Little information exists about how they are funded or paid. Across states, the share of volunteers ranges from 16 percent (Eastern Equatoria) to 68 percent (Jonglei). The 10 states are the employers of the frontline staff and are therefore responsible for managing most of the public education spending. There are wide disparities in the resources available to the states, however. For example, *staff are not distributed across the states consistent with enrollments, and it seems states are able to pay widely different average salaries with the resources they receive.* The end result is widely different levels of average per student spending in both primary and secondary schools.

Public per student spending is SDG 118 in primary school, SDG 349 in secondary school, and SDG 1,555 in higher education, on average (table 1). The primary per student spending, which corresponds to about 11 percent of GDP per capita, is comparable with the level of spending observed in other SSA countries that are at a similar level of income. This is also true for the other two levels of education.

Table 1 Public per Student Spending by Level of Education, 2009 (SDG)

Level of education	Per student salary spending		Per student operating spending	Total per student spending	
	School-based staff	Nonschool-based staff		SDG	Multiples of primary
Primary	67 (57%)	26 (22%)	25 (21%)	118	1
Secondary	181 (52%)	94 (27%)	74 (21%)	349	3
Higher education	1,555 (71%)		628 (29%)	2,183	19

Source: World Bank estimation.

There are still primary school fees in some states, but not much is known about fees, or about whether parents are funding the many volunteer teachers. In the most recent household survey, parents reported fairly moderate amounts of yearly education spending. More information is needed to determine whether school fees are limiting access to school for some children.

ARE THE RESOURCES WELL DEPLOYED AND MANAGED TO ENSURE EFFICIENT FUNCTIONING OF THE EDUCATION SYSTEM?

School inputs are not distributed equally across states; this means that schools in some states receive far less school inputs than average for South Sudan. The average pupil-teacher ratio varies between 31 in Central Equatoria and 84 in Jonglei (excluding volunteer teachers, the range is from 44 in Central Equatoria to 139 in Jonglei). Clearly, those attending school in Jonglei and Unity and several other states are not benefiting from even minimally adequate schooling conditions. The problem, however, is not so much the total level of schooling inputs as the distribution of them.

The distribution of resources across schools is also poor. The average pupil-teacher ratio says very little about the actual situation in schools, as teachers are not distributed across schools proportionally to enrollments (figure 5). Excluding the outliers, schools with 500 pupils can have anywhere between 1 and 20 teachers, and, similarly, schools with 6 teachers can have enrollments anywhere between 50 and 800 pupils. Textbooks and classrooms are also poorly distributed across schools.

The teacher workforce is a critical component of primary and secondary education. *Significant strides have been made in establishing a functioning payroll system for teachers and other education sector staff in the states.* Teachers' knowledge of subject content is weak, which reflects the limited academic and professional training received. The number of ade-

Figure 5   Consistency between Number of Teachers and Pupils in Government Primary Schools, 2009

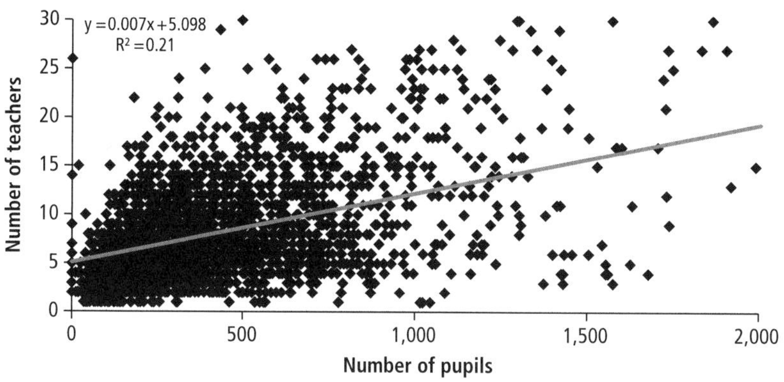

Source: Analysis of EMIS 2009.
Note: The figure is based on government schools only. Each dot or observation represents a school. The number of teachers includes volunteer teachers.

quately trained teachers in primary education is low in South Sudan. Forty-six percent of teachers have only a primary school education and another 45 percent have secondary certification. About 61 percent of teachers do not possess any professional training to be teachers. Upgrading the disciplinary and pedagogical knowledge of teachers presents an urgent task for South Sudan. Of particular concern is the low proportion of female teachers in both primary and secondary education—less than 15 percent. Presently, women make up 24 percent of enrollments in the primary teacher training colleges, so the share of female teachers is only set to increase slowly. In addition, allocating teachers in a salary grade is a challenge because of the lack of verifiable information on teachers' backgrounds. The academic and professional background for a small number of teachers is also unknown, which makes this exercise even more difficult.

An effectively managed teaching force is critical to regular school functioning and instructional quality. Teacher management policies in South Sudan are evolving and will require concerted efforts to develop, pilot, and fine tune. *Implementing clear recruitment, deployment, and transfer policies that can guide and strengthen the teaching force will be critical*. In addition, establishing a supervision system that monitors teachers' work will also serve to support and sustain good performance.

Unclear policies and weak supervision effectively limit the instructional time offered to students. There is no clear policy on the number of working days in a school year, and some schools function for less than eight months a year. Furthermore, there is no uniform record keeping associated with enrollment, student performance, and teachers' leave. The slow coverage of the syllabus in classrooms points to a shortage of instructional time, limiting what students learn each year.

CONCLUSIONS

This report points to the following priority areas that deserve the particular attention of policy makers and the public:

South Sudan will need to add capacity to the education system to reach UPC, but in an increasingly selective and strategic manner. For example, the government will need to weigh the relative value of building additional classrooms for existing schools (because of the many incomplete schools) and building new schools. Furthermore, access to school is uneven by state and thus expansion strategies will need to be targeted.

Achieving UPC will mean increasing retention. There are already a very large number of youth in South Sudan who will never receive formal education; another large group will not finish their basic education. Only about a third of children who enroll in grade 1 are still in school by the end of the primary cycle. Access to the early grades is steadily increasing, but overall UPC is not increasing in step. Some of this problem may be due to the absence of classrooms at higher grades. Improving retention within primary education will require adding more grades to schools, at least up to grade 6. However, there are certainly other causes that must be identified and addressed, particularly considering that girls and the poorer populations are most apt to drop out of school.

The AES will continue to play a central part in the overall education system and deserves to be treated as such. The AES is a unique aspect of the education system. In the long run, it may become obsolete, if South Sudan is successful in achieving UPC. The chance that a child will sooner or later access some schooling is around 60 percent, up from about 40 percent a decade ago. However, this is still far from the 100 percent needed to attain UPC. For now and into the foreseeable future, AES will remain the second most important part of the education system. The tremendous number of out-of-school youths will continue to need educational opportunities that can only be provided by the AES. Generally, the AES has gained a good reputation among partners and the population. Further reinforcement of the quality and measurement of outcomes of this part of the education system should be a key pillar of ongoing government education strategy.

Gender inequity is a central feature of South Sudan's education system, particularly in the rural areas, but rural boys are also at a disadvantage. In urban areas where the educational coverage is relatively high, the gender inequity is diminishing. In rural areas, where educational coverage is much lower, all children are at a disadvantage compared with children in the cities, but girls more so than boys. Building more schools in rural areas closer to children's homes will expand educational opportunities for all rural children, but those that have most to gain are the girls. In most SSA countries, policies to expand the supply of fee-free primary education have been successful at getting most children to school. Supply-side policies, however, may not be sufficient to reach the most marginalized, such as children from very poor families.

South Sudan will need more teachers and more pedagogical inputs, but these must be better managed. It is clear that government-paid teachers are not deployed in an objective manner, considering that there appears to be little relationship between the number of students and the number of teachers in a given establishment. This is also true of the distribution of textbooks in the country. Any strategy to lower student-teacher ratios or raise textbook-student ratios must ensure that each additional teacher deployed and each additional book distributed contribute to reverse this inefficiency.

Although education expenditures on the whole are in line with international standards, the distribution of resources across states is uneven. The government has given due priority to the development of primary education, and current levels of per student spending are quite balanced. However, analysis also shows that resources are not equitably distributed across states within South Sudan. It also finds that schools do not have sufficient numbers of paid staff but rely on a large number of volunteers. Government resources made available for the recruitment and deployment of teachers do not appear to be equitably distributed. Student unit costs vary from one state to another, reflecting both the differential pay of teachers and the proportion of teaching staff that are volunteers (and thus paid "off-budget").

The quality of education in South Sudan must become a central consideration early on in the development of the education system. Low quality is not surprising considering the state of the education system at the time of the CPA. With the government racing to meet demand for schooling, quality may be temporarily sacrificed. However, continuing delays to increasing quality is a fundamental error committed by many countries as they expand their education system that is very difficult to reverse. The findings of different achievement tests are quite telling in this regard—both for students and for teachers. The determinants of poor achievement have yet to be identified for South Sudan. However, the undertraining of the teacher corps, the lack of basic education materials at the school level, and the inequitable distribution of educational resources are evident contributing factors.

The future development of the education sector in South Sudan will require greater accountability at all levels, which in turn means better and more widely available information about sector trends. This is not just a reflection of the analysts who conducted this exhaustive study of education in the country. It is evident that if policies are to be effectively developed and implemented, much more reliable and detailed data will be needed in order to determine the trade-offs between policy options, measure results, and hold the education system accountable to the people of South Sudan.

NOTES

1. In some instances in this report, Republic of South Sudan has been shortened to South Sudan.

2. A test of student learning achievement in language and mathematics was administered to 1,800 students in primary schools in the states of Central Equatoria, Lakes, Upper Nile, and Western Bahr Ghazal. The test was given to students in grade 6 in 107 schools across the four states in July/August of 2010. The sample included mainly urban schools.

CHAPTER 1

Background and Context

The purpose of this Education Status Report (ESR), titled *Education in the Republic of South Sudan: Status and Challenges for a New System*, is to provide an overview of the education system in the Republic of South Sudan[1] on the eve of independence. It describes the state and key recent trends of the education sector, with a particular focus on primary education.

This report is the product of a collaborative process between the Ministry of Education (MoE) of the Government of the Republic of South Sudan (GoRSS) and a World Bank team. The ESR was launched in 2009 and a first workshop to discuss preliminary results was held in Juba in February of 2010 with the participation of MoE and donor representatives. A second workshop, held in Juba in October of 2010, presented more elaborate results to the new administration following the April elections. Finally, in February of 2011, shortly after the referendum, the team presented the close-to-final results at a large workshop in Juba that was chaired by the Minister of Education, and attended by more than 50 participants, who endorsed the results of the report.

BACKGROUND

Since Sudan's independence from Anglo-Egyptian rule in 1956 and until the signing of the Comprehensive Peace Agreement (CPA) in 2005, the Republic of South Sudan was at the center of two long-lasting civil wars (the first from 1955 to 1972 and the second from 1983 to 2005), which affected every aspect of Sudanese life, including educational opportunities. At present, at only 27 percent (NBHS 2009), South Sudan has one of the lowest rates of adult literacy in the world today.[2] Since the signing of the CPA and implementation of its power- and wealth-sharing protocols, the education system has been under significant transformation. For the first time, a coordinated education system is being put in place supported by public resources to serve the entire population of South Sudan.

DEMOGRAPHIC, GEOGRAPHICAL, AND POLITICAL CONTEXT

The population of South Sudan was 8.3 million in the 2008 Census (SSCCSE 2008). The population of all of Sudan was 39.2 million, a four-fold increase from the 10.3 million inhabitants recorded in 1956, the year of Sudan's first population census. The population growth rate in Sudan remains high, particularly in South Sudan, where it is likely between 2 and 3 percent per year, on average. Between 2004 and 2008, some 1.8 million internally displaced person (IDPs) and refugees returned to South Sudan, according to its first statistical yearbook, and more people are expected to return from abroad as a result of independence (SSCCSE 2010a).[3]

Map 1.1   The Republic of South Sudan

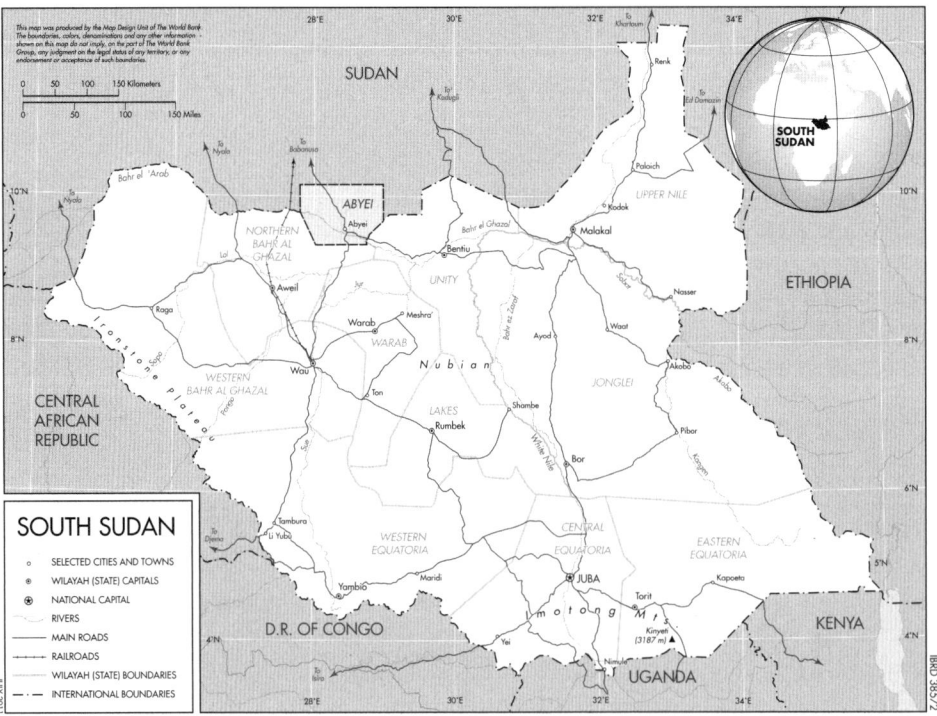

Source: World Bank.

South Sudan has a large territory with a low population density. At 644,000 square kilometers, South Sudan became the 42nd largest country in the world and the 15th largest country in Sub-Saharan Africa upon independence. The population density is only 13 inhabitants per square kilometer, a comparatively low number from an international perspective (the world average is about 50). It is landlocked and shares borders with the Democratic Republic of Congo, the Central African Republic, Ethiopia, Kenya, the Republic of Sudan, and Uganda (see map 1.1).

Administratively, South Sudan is divided into 10 states, which are subdivided into counties and further divided into *payams* and *bomas*. Table 1.1 lists the population, area, and population density of each of the 10 states. The two most populous states, Central Equatoria—home to Juba, the capital of South Sudan—and Jonglei, each have more than 1 million inhabitants. Central Equatoria is the most densely populated state. With only a little over 300,000 inhabitants, Western Bahr Ghazal is the state with the smallest population and the lowest population density.

The signing of the Comprehensive Peace Agreement in 2005 led to the formation of the GoRSS, which has governed the region for the past six years with extensive autonomy over the country's affairs. Following the independence referendum of January 2011, the Republic of South Sudan became an independent state on July 9, 2011. GoRSS has gradually established own institutions, including a Ministry of Education, Science and

Table 1.1   Population of the Republic of South Sudan by State, 2008

State	Population	% of total population	Area (km²)	Population density
Jonglei	1,358,602	16	122,581	11
Central Equatoria	1,103,592	13	43,033	26
Warrap	972,928	12	45,566	21
Upper Nile	964,353	12	77,283	12
Eastern Equatoria	906,126	11	73,472	12
Northern Bahr Ghazal	720,898	9	30,543	24
Lakes	695,730	8	43,595	16
Western Equatoria	619,029	7	79,343	8
Unity	585,801	7	37,837	15
Western Bahr Ghazal	333,431	4	91,076	4
Total	8,260,490	100	644,329	13

Source: SSCCSE (2010a).

Technology (MoEST), which was reorganized as two ministries in 2010: the Ministry of Education (MoE) and the Ministry of Higher Education, Science and Technology (MoHEST).

States, through their state ministries of education (SMoEs), have direct responsibility for operating public primary and secondary schools and Alternative Education System (AES) centers. Their responsibilities include, among others, hiring of teachers and other school-based staff, payroll administration, and disbursement of salaries. The funds for teachers' salaries are received from GoRSS in the form of the "conditional education transfer." These are funds dedicated to salaries for education sector staff. The funds received from GoRSS are not sufficient to pay all staff in the public schools, which continue to employ many staff who are not on government payroll. Often referred to as volunteers, these staff are likely paid from fees collected from parents.

Figure 1.1 zooms in on the population aged 24 and younger based on the raw 2008 population census data. The uneven pattern of the data reflects that many parents report the approximate age of their children (which tends to be easier, rounded numbers such as 10, 20, and so forth) rather than their exact age. For the purposes of this report, the raw 2008 population data were smoothed as explained in appendix B, which also provides tables with the resulting population data used in the report.

Figure 1.1 Raw Census Data on Population by Age in the Republic of South Sudan, 2008

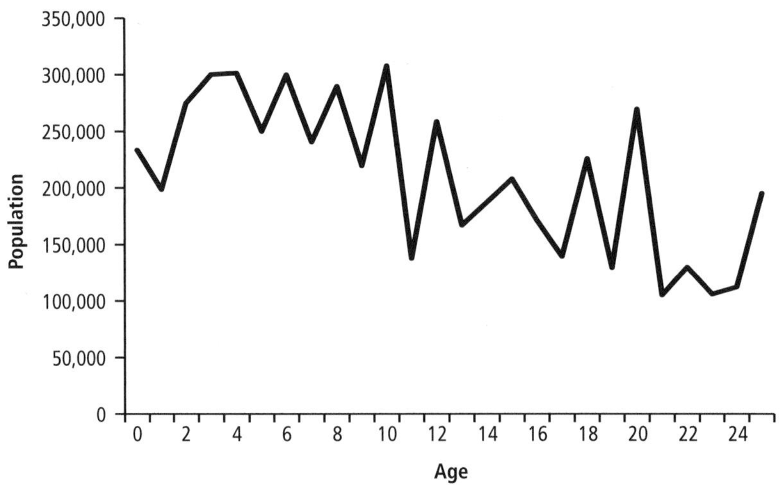

Source: 2008 Population Census.

Providing basic education for all under strong demographic pressure is a real challenge. In South Sudan, 33.1 percent of the population was between the ages of 5 and 16 in 2008. This makes the demographic context of South Sudan on par with many Sub-Saharan African countries (average of 34.4 percent). However, as figure 1.2 shows, the population is growing rapidly: there are about twice as many 2-year-olds as 21-year-olds. This has clear implications for the education system, because the growth of the education system will need to accommodate increasingly larger age cohorts. The many returnees add to the demographic pressure and to the challenge of providing basic services of an acceptable quality to all.

In terms of expected demographic growth in the next few years, the ESR team estimates that total population growth will be around 2.4 percent per year, with the primary school-age population growing at about 2.2 percent per year.[4]

MACROECONOMIC CONTEXT

At the time of writing, macroeconomic indicators, such as GDP, are not yet available for South Sudan. Data for Sudan before the 2011 independence of South Sudan point to strong economic growth since the mid-

Figure 1.2 Age Structure of Population (Ages 2–24), the Republic of South Sudan, 2009

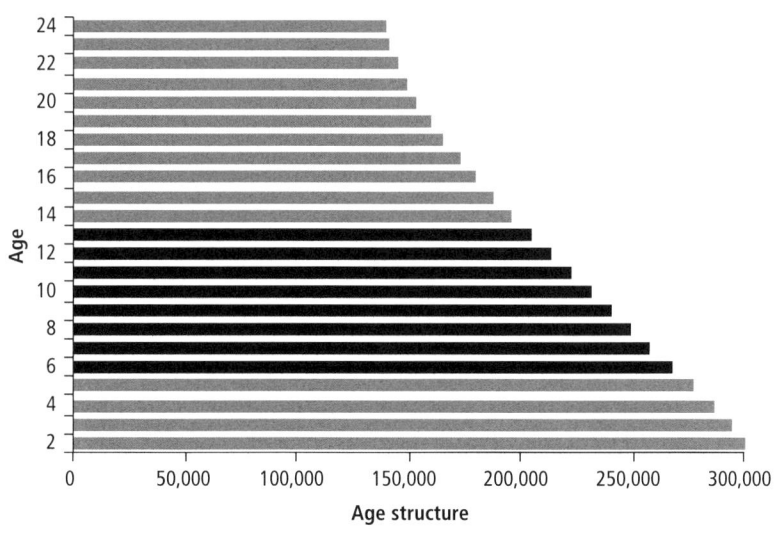

Source: World Bank projection based on 2008 Population Census.

1990s, particularly since 1999 when Sudan started exporting oil in significant amounts (World Bank 2009). Between 1995 and 2008, Sudan's GDP grew by a factor of 2.5 from US$22 billion to US$55 billion (in constant 2009 U.S. dollars). Over the same period, the GDP per capita—a measure of average income per person—almost doubled in real terms, from US$708 per capita in 1995 to more than US$1,294 per capita in 2009 (both in constant 2009 U.S. dollars) (figure 1.3).

South Sudan's economy was traditionally less developed than that of the north, but economic growth has picked up since the CPA as a result of peace and reconstruction efforts, oil revenue, and donor support (although data documenting these trends are scarce). South Sudan is a predominantly rural economy with 83 percent of the population residing in rural areas. Agriculture (crops and livestock) is the main source of livelihood for 78 percent of the country's households. The war left the region with virtually no infrastructure (World Bank 2009), but substantial construction and rehabilitation have taken place since the CPA, despite considerable capacity issues in the construction sector (Hjort 2008). Further, essential institutions have been established, such as government institutions and banks, and many small businesses have been set up, mainly in the 10 state capitals (SSCCSE 2010b).

For this report, a rough estimate of South Sudan's GDP per capita was calculated.[5] This was estimated at SDG 1,114 for 2009 (equivalent to US$484 per person).[6] GDP for the oil and non-oil sectors was estimated separately based on GoRSS revenues from oil and non-oil, respectively. For the oil sector, it was assumed that GoRSS' oil revenues make up 50

Figure 1.3 Trend in Sudan's GDP per Capita, 1975–2009

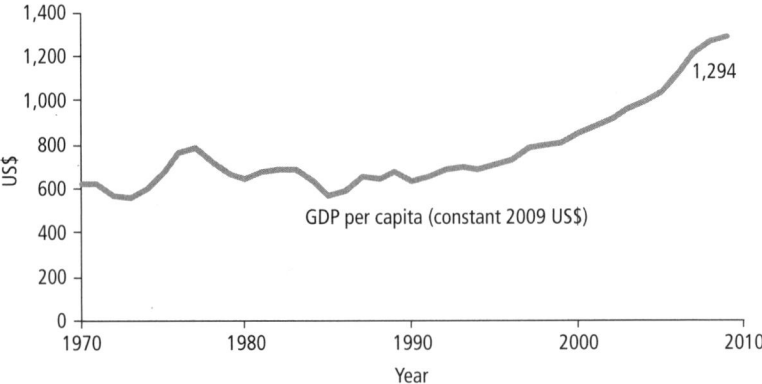

Source: Data from World Bank's World Development Indicator (WDI) database (http://data.worldbank.org/data-catalog/world-development-indicators).

percent of South Sudan's oil sector GDP to account for the cost of oil extraction (50 percent) that would be deducted before revenue payout. For the non-oil sector, it was assumed that GoRSS' non-oil revenues are 10 percent of South Sudan's non-oil GDP—that is, that the tax pressure in the non-oil sector is 10 percent.

POVERTY AND SOCIAL DEVELOPMENT CONTEXT

South Sudan is one of the least developed countries in the world and poverty is widespread. The recently completed poverty assessment (SSCCSE 2010c) estimates that the monthly per capita consumption in South Sudan was SDG 100 in 2009 (corresponding to US$43 per month or US$522 per year).[7] On average, 51 percent of the population falls below the national poverty line of SDG 72.9 per person per month (in 2009).

Most of the population is illiterate, although younger generations are much more likely to be literate than older generations, as illustrated in figure 1.4. This is a result of the expansion of educational coverage over the past decade or so. On average for those 15 and older, the literacy rate is 39 percent for men and 15 percent for women, for an average adult literacy rate of 27 percent. The literacy rate peaks at about 60 percent for boys and at about 40 percent for girls.

South Sudan has some of the worst indicators of health and human development of any country. In 2005, there were an estimated 2,054 maternal deaths per 100,000 live births, which places South Sudan along-

Figure 1.4 Literacy Rate by Age and Gender, 2009

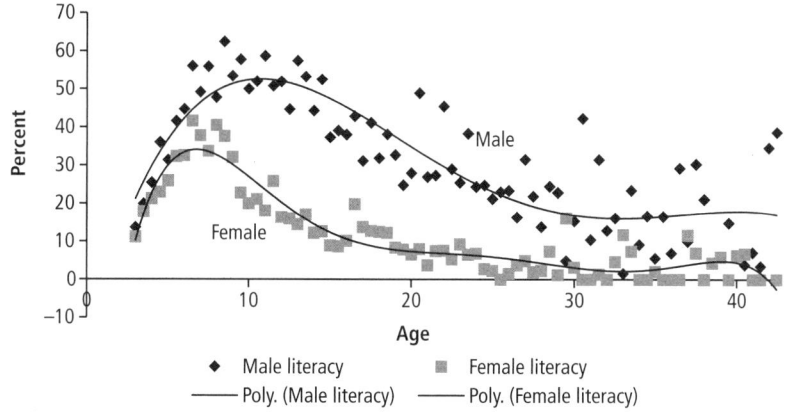

Source: Analysis of NBHS 2009.
Note: The figure shows survey observations and the polynomial (Poly. in the above figure) curves that best fit the data.

side Sierra Leone, Afghanistan, and Niger as the places with the highest maternal mortality rates in the world. This is likely associated with the comparatively low coverage of professional care during delivery in South Sudan. The country's under-five mortality rate is also high and did not show any sign of improvement between 1980 and 2005. An estimated 14 children out of every 100 will not survive to their fifth birthday, most of them dying from preventable causes. A recent World Bank report found striking variations in these mortality rates across states and quintiles of wealth in South Sudan (World Bank 2011c).

In the health sector, existing public health infrastructure collapsed during the war and health services were delivered mainly through nongovernmental organizations (NGOs) and UN agencies operating emergency relief programs. Although significant progress has been made in terms of strengthening the health system since the CPA, in particular the creation and staffing of the central and state ministries of health and the development of key policy documents (including the central government's Basic Package of Health Services) that provide the vision and values underpinning the health system, much work remains. The 2009 National Baseline Household Survey (NBHS) showed that 69 percent of households have access to some health services, but also that many of those that do visit a health facility pay out of pocket for care (World Bank 2011c).

Table 1.2 provides some key data for each of the 10 states in South Sudan. The table shows considerable disparities across the states with respect to poverty incidence, from 26 percent in Upper Nile to 76 percent in North Bahr Ghazal. It also shows substantial variation in the adult literacy rate, from 15 percent in Jonglei to 45 percent in Upper Nile. Similarly, the maternal mortality rate varies between 1,844 in Eastern Equatoria and 2,326 maternal deaths per 100,000 live births in Western Equatoria. In North Bahr Ghazal, 23 out of 100 children will not survive to their fifth birthday, while this is the case for 7 children out of 100 in Unity. Finally, the table shows a moderate variation in the share of the population that is between the ages of 5 and 16, from 30 percent in Western Equatoria to 36 percent in Eastern Equatoria.

TRENDS IN GOVERNMENT REVENUES AND EXPENDITURES

GoRSS has fairly large domestic revenues for a postconflict country, mostly from oil (World Bank 2009). Table 1.3 shows total GoRSS revenue and expenditure between 2006 and 2010.[8] Revenue totaled SDG 4.2 billion in 2009 or about SDG 501 per person (equivalent to US$218 per capita). This fairly high level of domestic revenue for a postconflict coun-

Table 1.2 Population and Poverty Incidence by State, 2009

Population and incidence	CEQ	EEQ	Jonglei	Lakes	NBG	Unity	Upper Nile	Warrap	WBG	WEQ	Total
Population age 5–16 as share of total pop. (%)	32	36	34	33	32	34	33	33	31	30	33
Consumption per person per month, 2009 (SDG)	128	103	98	108	60	71	144	69	114	107	100
Poverty incidence, 2009 (%)	44	50	48	49	76	68	26	64	43	42	51
Under-five mortality, 2005 (per thousand)	112	142	134	144	229	74	97	162	128	211	135
Maternal mortality, 2005 (per 100,000)	1,867	1,844	1,861	2,243	2,182	1,732	2,094	2,173	2,216	2,327	2,054
Adult literacy (age 15+)	44	19	15	17	21	26	45	16	34	33	27

Sources: Population data are from the 2008 Census. Poverty, consumption, and literacy data are based on NBHS 2009. Under-five mortality rates are from World Bank (2011b), based on the 2006 Sudan Household Health Survey (SHHS). Maternal mortality rates are from SSCCSE (2010a), also based on the 2006 SHHS.
Note: CEQ = Central Equatoria; EEQ = Eastern Equatoria; NBG = Northern Bahr el Ghazal; WBG = Western Bahr el Ghazal; WEQ = Western Equatoria.

Table 1.3 GoRSS Revenue and Expenditure, 2006–10 (in current SDG millions)

Source	2006 Actual	2007 Actual	2008 Actual	2009 Provisional	2010 Draft budget
Total GoRSS revenue	2,736.1	2,977.8	6,789.6	4,239.8	4,502.8
Oil revenue	2,732.9	2,964.5	6,670.9	4.121.5	4,401.8
Non-oil revenue	3.2	13.3	118.7	118	101
% from oil	100%	100%	98%	97%	98%
Total GoRSS expenditure	3,581.5	2,936.5	5,712.7	4,234.7	4,482.8
Recurrent	2,623.9	2,538.2	4,100.7	3,232.7	3,492.6
Capital	957.6	398.3	1,611.9	1,002.0	990.2
% recurrent	73%	86%	72%	76%	78%
Memo item:					
Transfer to states	525.5	631.6	637.6	1,089.9	1,227.9
% of expenditure	15%	22%	11%	26%	27%

Source: MOFEP budget books.

try is mainly funded by the oil revenue, which accounted for 97 percent of GoRSS' total revenue in 2009. The high dependency on oil renders GoRSS' budget very vulnerable to fluctuations in production levels and oil prices. Figure 1.5 shows the trend in GoRSS revenue and expenditure in real terms (in constant 2009 SDG million). With the exception of 2008, when a spike in oil prices resulted in exceptionally high revenue and expenditure, these have both remained relatively flat over the five-year period. Flat revenue and expenditure are painful in an environment of strong population growth, as they translate into lower per capita expenditures. In 2009, in particular, GoRSS revenues were hard hit by the global financial crisis, although they recovered somewhat in 2010.

Figure 1.5 also shows that a considerable share of GoRSS expenditure is transferred to the 10 states, and that this share has generally been growing since 2006, reaching 26 percent in 2009 and 27 percent in the 2010 budget. The states receive both block transfers to cover the cost of local government administration and earmarked, or "conditional," transfers for sectors such as education, health, infrastructure, natural resources and rural development, and others. Education receives one of the largest conditional transfers.

ORGANIZATION OF THE EDUCATION STATUS REPORT

Chapter 2 looks at overall patterns of student enrollments, while chapter 3 provides a more detailed analysis of student flow patterns. Chapter 4

Figure 1.5 Trends in GoRSS Revenues and Expenditures, 2006–10 (in constant 2009 SDG million)

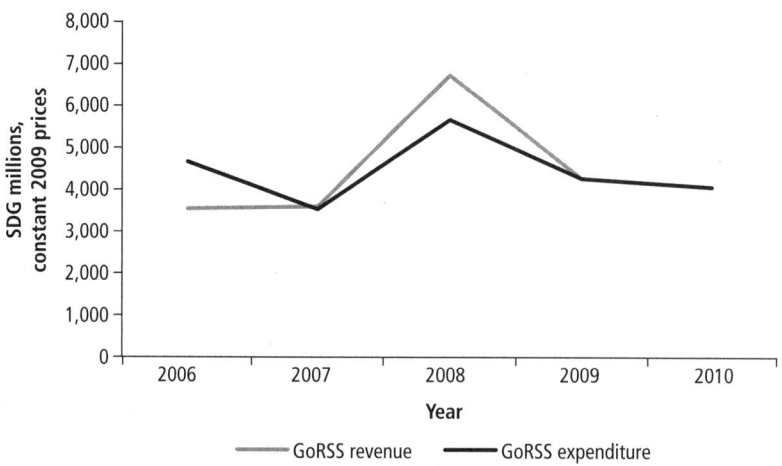

Source: Analysis of MOFEP budget books.

analyzes disparities in school participation across states and for boys and girls, urban and rural, and rich and poor. Chapter 5 analyzes service delivery and student learning achievement based on survey data. Chapter 6 focuses on the cost and financing of education in South Sudan. Chapter 7 provides an analysis of teacher policies and management, and chapter 8 offers some conclusions. Appendix F provides two-page data sheets with key indicators for each of the 10 states.

REPORT LIMITATIONS

This report has been prepared while a new education system has been in formation. By definition this means that current data were not always available or reliable. Fortunately, the GoRSS, with the support of the United States Agency for International Development (USAID) and the United Nations Children's Fund (UNICEF), had the foresight to invest early in the development of an education management information system (EMIS). Although still in its early phase, the data collected by EMIS are one of the principal sources of information for this report. Starting in 2007, education censuses have been carried out every year, from 2008 onwards also covering secondary schools and the Alternative Education System (AES). Every year, EMIS has been achieving better coverage of schools and learning spaces, thereby gradually improving the quality of the data; however, it will take more time before a reliable data source for education decision making will be fully in place.

The information available from the nascent EMIS is reinforced by household surveys and administrative data such as the states' payroll database. However, the different data sources can also be inconsistent. Caution has been taken throughout the analysis to compare data from different sources and work with the most consistent data sets. When there is a particularly large inconsistency, this is mentioned explicitly in the text. Nevertheless, by triangulating existing data sources, the authors believe that the ESR provides a faithful depiction of the state of education in South Sudan. They are confident that the report provides a firm foundation for the establishment of an education system that will provide equitable and good-quality education for all the people of South Sudan.

Although the overall focus of the study is sectorwide, the report provides relatively more information about primary schooling than about other levels of education. This is for the most part a result of more and better data being available about primary education. EMIS, for example, provides the most detailed information about primary schooling, thereby reflecting the incipient nature of the education system (and of EMIS itself) in the newly independent Republic of South Sudan. The relative focus on primary education, however, limits the scope of the conclusions that can be made about other levels of education.

NOTES

1. In some instances in this report, Republic of South Sudan has been shortened to South Sudan.

2. Of all the countries in the world that report their adult literacy rate, only Burkina Faso, Mali, and Niger also have adult literacy rates below 30 percent.

3. SSCCSE (2010a). The origin of the data is the Southern Sudan Relief and Rehabilitation Commission.

4. This is based on studying the age composition of the 2008 census population and by looking at United Nations (UN) population projections for Sudan. These growth rates could be used in short-term projections of the school-age population for purposes of assessing resource needs in the sector. For longer-term projections, slightly lower population growth rates would be expected.

5. This estimate was prepared for the purpose of international comparisons of education indicators, and should not be used for other purposes.

6. For comparison, the GDP for all of Sudan was about SDG 2,975 per capita in 2009.

7. The average per capita consumption is thus higher than our estimated GDP per capita. However, much of the food consumption in the Republic of South Sudan comes from households' own agricultural production. Since it is not traded, it would likely not fully enter the GDP. This could explain the discrepancy.

8. GoRSS was established around mid-2005, so 2006 was its first full fiscal year.

Overall Enrollment Patterns

This chapter reviews recent trends and patterns in student enrollments in the Republic of South Sudan. The chapter goes on to calculate the gross enrollment rates (GER) for each level of education and compare the levels of schooling coverage with those of other Sub-Saharan African (SSA) countries. Further, the chapter presents data on the organization of schools and learning places.

STRUCTURE OF THE EDUCATION SYSTEM

Historically, the education system in South Sudan was underdeveloped. Sommers (2005) provides a detailed account of the history of education in Sudan in the 1900s and particularly during the second civil war that lasted from 1983 to 2004. Although there was some growth in student enrollments before and during this period, the education sector was never very developed in South Sudan and investments in education remained low. That explains why this country has one of the lowest rates of adult literacy in the world today—27 percent based on the most recent household survey (NBHS 2009). Of all the countries in the world that report their adult literacy rate, only Burkina Faso, Mali, and Niger have adult literacy rates below 30 percent. Furthermore, the relatively few schools operating in South Sudan were not part of a coordinated education system. During the second civil war, for example, most schools were mission schools or run by communities or nongovernmental organizations (NGOs). Schools differed widely on almost all counts: duration of the primary and secondary cycles, curriculum (Ethiopian, Kenyan, Sudanese, Ugandan), language of instruction (English, Arabic), mode of organization, pupil-teacher ratios, and so forth.

In recent years—for the first time—a coordinated education system is under construction in South Sudan. Toward the end of the second civil war, the Sudan People's Liberation Movement (SPLM) started focusing on organizing schools, often with demobilized soldiers as teachers, but teachers received no formal pay. Since the signing of the Comprehensive Peace Agreement (CPA) in 2005 and implementation of its power- and wealth-sharing protocols, the education system is now under significant transformation. For the first time, a coordinated education system is being put in place supported by public resources to fund teachers. This is allowing for a very significant expansion of access to education, as we shall see in this chapter.

Although not yet used by all schools, South Sudan's education system is structured around (a) a system of formal education consisting of eight years of primary school and four years of secondary school followed by higher education (often four years), and (b) a system of nonformal education, known as the Alternative Education System (AES), that provides literacy education to individuals of all ages. In practice, the implementation of this system is still incomplete, as most primary and secondary schools are not yet offering the complete cycles.

Since the CPA the Government of the Republic of South Sudan (GoRSS), with the support of the United States Agency for International Development (USAID) and the United Nations Children's Fund (UNICEF), started rolling out the Education Management Information System (EMIS). This process started in 2006 with the Rapid Assessment of Learning Spaces (RALS) survey of primary schools. Starting in 2007, education censuses have been carried out every year, from 2008 onwards also covering secondary schools and AES. Year by year the EMIS is achieving better coverage of schools and learning spaces, thereby gradually improving the quality of the data. The completeness of the EMIS education census, in terms of share of participating schools, is discussed in detail in the EMIS National Statistical Booklet for the 2009 school year (MoE-EMIS 2010).

Two state ministries of education (SMoE) also collect their own educational statistics: Eastern Equatoria and Lakes.

TREND IN STUDENT ENROLLMENTS

There are no official, definitive data on school enrollments for the years before 2005, but several estimates are available. From 2005 onwards, data sources gradually grew more reliable. Appendix C presents data from several sources for an overview of enrollments over the five years before the CPA (table C.1) and for the 2005–09 period (table C.2).

Table 2.1 Average Growth in Student Enrollments, by Level, 2000–09

Level	2000	2005	2009	Average annual enrollment growth (%)		
				2000–05	2005–09	2000–09
Primary education	331,000	669,000	1,380,580	15	20	17
Secondary education	7,740	17,465	44,027	18	26	21
Higher education	15,102 (2002)		23,968			7 (2002–09)
Vocational training	724		2,760			16

Sources: Data from table C.1 and table C.2.

Primary school enrollments have risen spectacularly in South Sudan over the past decade: they approximately doubled between 2000 and 2005 from 0.3 million to 0.7 million, and then again between 2005 and 2009 from 0.7 million to 1.4 million (table 2.1). Thus, the more peaceful and stable period since 2000, and in particular since 2005, has facilitated a large growth in the student population. Secondary school enrollments also grew. EMIS records secondary school enrollments at 44,027 in 2009, the second year that such data were collected by school census. This is up from 7,740 in 2000 and 17,465 in 2005 (table 2.1).

Since 2005, primary school enrollments have grown by 20 percent per year, on average (compared with 15 percent per year between 2000 and 2005). Between 2005 and 2009, secondary school enrollments grew by an estimated 26 percent per year (compared with about 18 percent per year between 2000 and 2005). Finally, higher education enrollments grew at a more modest pace by about 7 percent per year since 2002. Primary schools have added more than a million students in nine years, most of them after 2005.

THE GROSS ENROLLMENT RATIO

The primary school GER[1] grew from 21 percent in 2000 to 72 percent in 2009. Figure 2.1 illustrates the trend in primary school enrollments and in the primary school-age population. As a result of demographic growth, we estimate that the school-age population has grown from about 1.5 million in 2000 to 1.9 million in 2009. Due to the much faster enrollment growth, the primary school GER has increased from an estimated 21 percent in 2000 to 72 percent in 2009, an impressive feat by any measure.

Figure 2.1 Trend in Primary School Enrollments, School-Age Population and GER, 2000–09

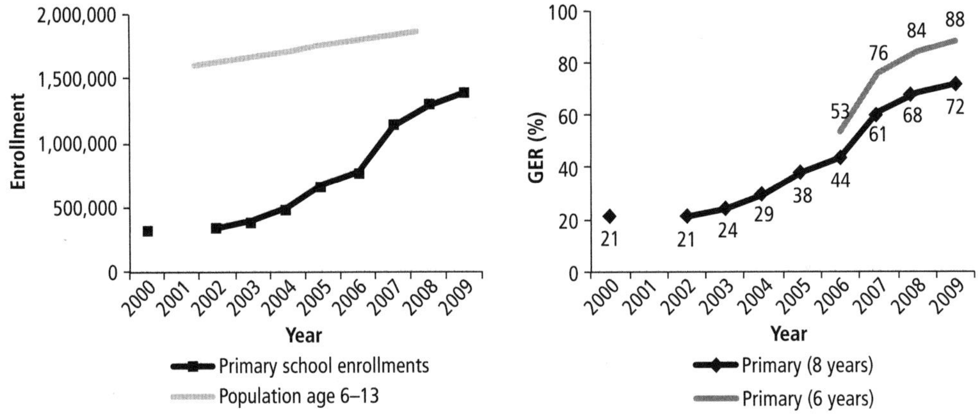

Source: Analysis based on data in appendixes B and C.

Focusing on the first six years of the primary cycle—the cycle length used in most international comparisons of primary education—the GER attained 88 percent in 2009.

This is significantly lower than the average primary school GER for Sub-Saharan Africa (SSA) (104 percent).[2] At 88 percent, South Sudan's primary GER (six years) is comparable, however, to that of a few other SSA countries, such as 90 percent in Chad, 89 percent in Central African Republic, and 90 percent in the Democratic Republic of Congo (table 2.2). In the years ahead, South Sudan's GER will likely also reach and exceed 100 percent for a number of years until the system stabilizes.

Table 2.2 International Comparison of Educational Coverage, 2009

Region	Primary (6 years) GER (%)	Upper secondary GER (%)	Higher No. of students per 100,000 inhabitants
Central African Republic	89	8	240
Chad	90	17	187
Congo, Dem. Rep.	90	31	591
Ethiopia	102	15	337
Kenya	113	43	433
Uganda	122	15	352
Sub-Saharan Africa[a]	104	29	572
The Republic of South Sudan	88	6	283

Sources: UNESCO Institute for Statistics (http://www.uis.unesco.org) and World Bank education country status reports.
a. Unweighted average.

Based on EMIS data on enrollments, secondary school GER is 6 percent in South Sudan, which is much lower than the average of 29 percent for Sub-Saharan Africa (table 2.2). It is also lower than levels found in several SSA countries close to South Sudan, such as the Central African Republic (8 percent), Chad (17 percent), and Uganda (15 percent).

Including enrollments at Khartoum campuses, the Republic of South Sudan has 283 university students per 100,000 inhabitants—half of the SSA average. In 2009, higher education enrollments totaled 23,968, although 73 percent of these were actually enrolled at the Khartoum campuses of South Sudan's universities (see also table 2.6 later in this chapter). This corresponds to a higher education GER of about 3.7 percent.[3] For comparative purposes, the average of this indicator for SSA countries is 572 students per 100,000 inhabitants; Chad has 187, Central African Republic has 240, the Democratic Republic of Congo has 591, and Uganda has 352 students per 100,000 inhabitants.

THE FORMAL EDUCATION SYSTEM: SCHOOL NETWORK AND ORGANIZATION

PRE-PRIMARY EDUCATION

Pre-primary education is at an early stage of development. Previously, the Ministry of Education (MoE) had not been collecting data on pre-primary enrollments, but started collecting and publicizing these data as of the 2010 school year. In 2009, the payroll database included a little over 400 government-paid staff that worked in 75 nursery schools, all in Central or Eastern Equatoria State. There are also private and NGO-supported early childhood development (ECD) or preschool centers; for instance, the Catholic Church reported enrolling as many as 4,738 students in kindergarten across South Sudan.

PRIMARY EDUCATION

Some 85 percent of primary schools operate with some public funding (figure 2.2). EMIS uses a typology of schools that reflects some combination of funding and management arrangement:

- Government schools are publicly funded and managed.
- Government-aided schools receive public funding but are privately managed (some by churches and mosques).
- Private schools are privately funded and managed (some by churches or mosques).

Figure 2.2 Primary Schools by Ownership and Funding, 2009

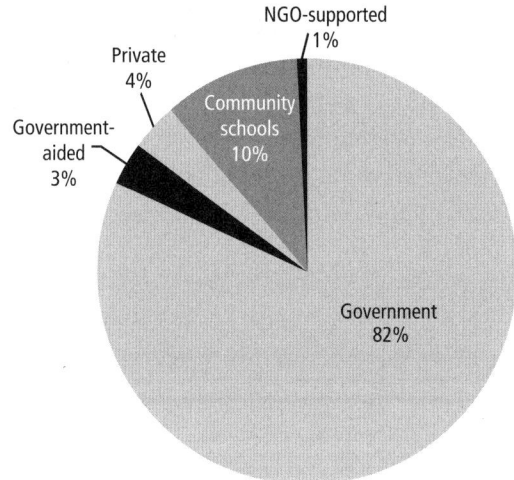

Source: Analysis of EMIS 2009.

- Community schools are funded and managed by communities without government support.
- NGO-supported schools are funded and managed by NGOs without government support.

The need to operate with so many school categories reflects that the boundaries between government and non-government schools are quite fluid. Goldsmith (2010), for example, describes how some church schools have church-, government-, and parent-paid teachers within the same institution. This arrangement allows government to have leverage across more than just government schools. Private profit-making schools are beginning to open in some larger towns in South Sudan for the first time.

According to EMIS, the majority of schools (85 percent) are either government schools or government-aided schools. This leaves 15 percent of schools that are funded from private sources. Enrollments are about 1,149,000 in government schools (83 percent of total), 51,000 in government-aided schools (4 percent), 59,000 in private schools (4 percent), 112,000 in community schools (8 percent), and 9,000 in NGO-supported schools (1 percent).

The average size of a primary school has doubled in just seven years. The strong growth in school enrollments has been accompanied by a considerable expansion of the school system, although the stock of schools has not kept up with enrollment growth. Table 2.3 shows that although

Table 2.3 Evolution in the Number of Primary Schools and School Size, 1980–2009

Year	Number of schools	Average enrollments per school
1980/81	~900	184
2002	~1,600	212
2006	2,922	259
2007	3,068	368
2008	3,195	402
2009	3,221	429

Sources: World Bank based on data from Brophy (2003) for 1980/81; from UNICEF (2004) for 2002; and the remaining data from MoE-EMIS (2010).

the number of primary schools has grown steadily, the average enrollments per school increased from 184 around 1980 to 212 by 2002 and as much as 429 students per primary school in 2009, a high number in a country with a predominantly rural population. The result is many overcrowded schools.

The average pupil-teacher ratio is 52 and increasing. Table 2.4 provides data on trends between 2007 and 2009. In that two-year interval, primary enrollments grew by 22 percent, but the number of schools grew only by 5 percent, and teachers only by 2 percent (the number of classrooms, however, grew by 62 percent). This led to an increase in the average pupil-teacher ratio from 43 in 2007 to 52 in 2009, including the volunteer

Table 2.4 Trend in the Organization of Primary Schools, 2007–09

Year	Enroll-ments	No. of schools	No. of teachers (incl. volunteers)	No. of classrooms (perm. or semi-perm.)	Teachers/ school (incl. volunteers)	Classrooms/ school (perm. or semiperm.)	Pupil-teacher ratio	Pupil-classroom ratio
2007	1,127,963	3,068	25,934	6,587	8.5	2.1	43	171
2008	1,284,252	3,195	25,912	6,611	8.1	2.1	50	194
2009	1,380,580	3,221	26,575	10,663	8.3	3.3	52	129
Index (2007=100)	122	105	102	162	—	—	—	—

Source: World Bank based MoE-EMIS (2010).
Note: — = Not available; perm = permanent.

teachers. Meanwhile the pupil-classroom ratio improved from 171 to 129. The table also shows that the average primary school in South Sudan has eight teachers and three classrooms in 2009, so classrooms are still in short supply despite progress made since 2007.

Fifteen percent of primary schools operate more than one shift. Schools with multiple shifts account for 20 percent of the student body in primary schools since multishift schools are considerably larger (553 students) than single-shift schools (377), on average. Multishift and single-shift schools have similar pupil-teacher ratios, so this mode of organization is used predominantly in schools with large enrollments to obtain a more efficient use of classrooms. Multishifting is unusual in the three Equatoria states (5–10 percent) but more common in states such as Warrap (24 percent), Northern Bahr Ghazal (22 percent), and Western Bahr Ghazal (19 percent). Classroom construction costs are high in South Sudan, particularly in states that have no or little local construction materials (these states tend to border northern Sudan).[4]

As many as 87 percent of primary schools are incomplete (figure 2.3). Although almost all schools offer grades 1 and 2, and most have grades 3 and 4, many fewer schools have grades 5 and above. Only 13 percent have a grade 8. Some may be new schools and only add one additional grade each year as the first cohort of students moves up through the grades. As mentioned in the previous section, some schools are not following the South Sudanese curriculum and offer only, for example, the Ugandan seven-year primary cycle. Nevertheless, the share of incomplete schools is very high and represents a principal constraint to attaining the MDG of universal primary completion (six years of schooling or more).

Figure 2.3 Share of Primary Schools that Offer Each of the Primary Grades, 2009

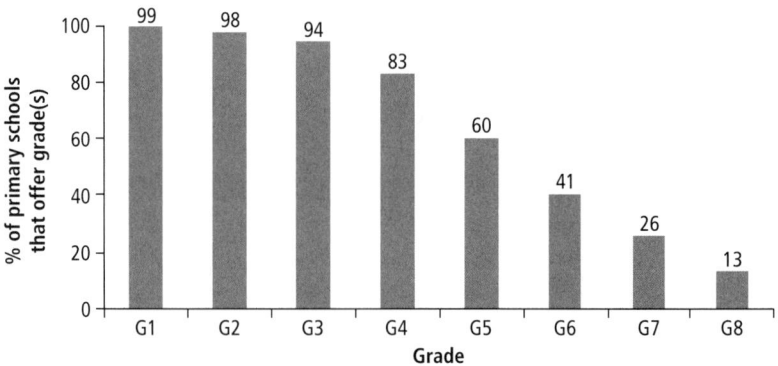

Source: Analysis of EMIS 2009.

Figure 2.4 Secondary Schools by Ownership, 2009

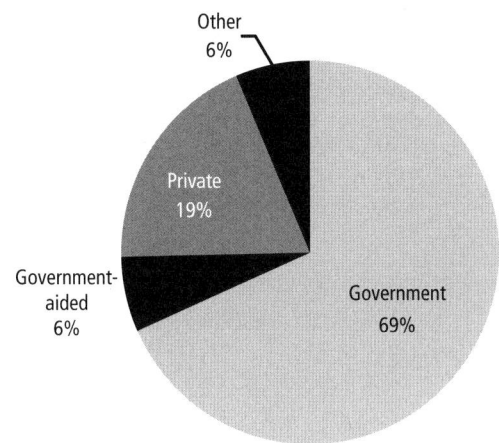

Source: Analysis of EMIS 2009.

SECONDARY EDUCATION

In secondary education, 75 percent of schools are publicly funded. In 2009, EMIS recorded 158 schools and an enrollment of 44,027. As in the primary subsector, most schools are government funded, although the secondary subsector has a slightly higher share of privately funded schools than the primary subsector (figure 2.4). The school census data reveal considerable variation in the educational offerings at secondary schools in 2009. Although the secondary school cycle is now officially four years, the majority of secondary schools offered less, whether only one grade (9 schools), two grades (25 schools), or three grades of secondary education (81 schools). Only 38 out of 158 secondary schools offered all four years of secondary school in 2009. Some of the schools with less than four grades may be new and may only add the final grades as students move up through the cycle. Others may still be operating under foreign curricula and thus offer three-year or six-year cycles. A number of schools still reported significant grade 6 enrollments in 2009 totaling as much as 27 percent of total secondary enrollments that year. This is a remainder of the six-year secondary cycle typically offered by secondary schools that followed the Kenyan or Ugandan system. However, very few were in grade 5 in 2009, so this practice is clearly being discontinued.

As shown in table 2.5, the average school has some 280 students, 14 teachers, and 6 nonteaching staff, but only 5 classrooms (permanent or semipermanent). The small number of classrooms points to fairly large class sizes. As shown, EMIS has registered 118 public secondary schools,

Table 2.5 Organization of Secondary Schools, Public and Private, 2009

School type	Enrollments	No. of schools	No. of teachers	No. of nonteaching staff	No. of classrooms[a]	Enrollments/ school	Teachers/ school	Classrooms/ school	Pupil-teacher ratio	Pupils per nonteaching staff	Pupil-classroom ratio
All schools	44,027	158	2,191	925	764	279	14	4.8	20	48	58
Public[b]	33,838	118	1,704	759	578	287	14	4.9	20	45	59
Private/other	10,189	40	487	166	186	255	12	4.7	21	61	55

Source: Analysis of EMIS 2009.
a. Permanent or semipermanent classrooms. b. Government or government-aided.

but the payroll database for the states counted 173 public secondary schools in 2009. Ten secondary schools have a special status as National Secondary Schools, and enjoy better funding than other government secondary schools. These elite schools are funded directly by the MoE and not through the states.

HIGHER EDUCATION

There are currently eight universities in South Sudan, three public and five private (and possibly more new private universities not included yet). The three public universities, Juba, Bahr El Ghazal, and Upper Nile University, each have one campus in South Sudan and one in northern Sudan. As set out in the CPA, the three public universities are mainly funded by the Government of National Unity in Khartoum. Juba University is by far the largest of the eight universities. It accounts for more than 60 percent of total higher education enrollments, although most of its students are in Khartoum.

Enrollments in higher education have grown from 15,102 students in 2002 to almost 24,000 students in 2009 (7 percent per year, on average), a fairly moderate increase compared with that of primary and secondary education (17 percent and 21 percent per year, respectively) (table 2.6).

Table 2.6 Higher Education Enrollments at the Republic of South Sudan's Universities (and Ownership, Campus Location), 2009

Campus location	Enrollments at the Republic of South Sudan campuses (e.g., Juba, Malakal, or Wau)	Enrollments at northern Sudan campuses (Khartoum)	Total higher education enrollments
Public			
Juba University	2,113	12,668	14,781
University of Bahr El Ghazal	1,666	3,316	4,982
Upper Nile University	1,608	1,407	3,065
Subtotal public universities	5,387	17,391	22,828
Private			
Catholic University of Sudan	352		352
Dr. John Garang Institute	142		142
Southern Sudan Open College	340		340
Sunshine Learning College	142		142
Upendo Christian University	164		164
Subtotal private universities	1,140		1,140
Total	**6,527**	**17,441**	**23,968**
% private enrollments	**17**	**0**	**5**

Sources: Juba University figures were collected directly from the university. Other figures are from MoE-EMIS (2010).

Enrollment figures may not reflect the total number of southerners attending university, however, as some attend other north Sudanese universities, and others may go abroad for their university studies.

Only 6,527 students are enrolled on South Sudan's campuses. Of these, 83 percent are enrolled in public universities and 17 percent in private institutions.

Figure 2.5 shows the enrollments by academic area at the Juba campus of Juba University. The three areas with the largest enrollments are rural development, education, and natural resources and environment. Next, figure 2.6 shows the breakdown of enrollments in the BSc program on the northern Sudan campuses of the three universities of the Republic of South Sudan: here, the three main areas are social sciences, education, and agriculture.

TECHNICAL/VOCATIONAL EDUCATION

Secondary-level vocational training is offered at some 20 vocational schools. Based on a total recorded enrollment of 2,625 students in 2009, the average school size was about 130 students. Vocational schools offer vocational training in a number of areas, including (in descending order by enrollments) tailoring, auto repair, carpentry, computers, masonry, electricity, welding, agriculture, plumbing, hair dressing, and printing. The centers also offer general education subjects including English and adult literacy.

Figure 2.5   Enrollments by Academic Area at the Juba Campus of Juba University, 2008–09

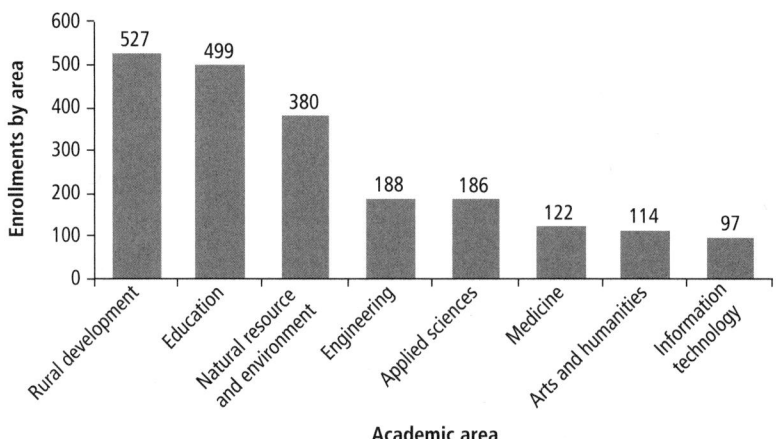

Source: Juba University.

Figure 2.6 Enrollments in the BSc Program by Academic Area at the Northern Sudan Campuses of Juba, Bahr El Ghazal, and Upper Nile Universities, 2009–10

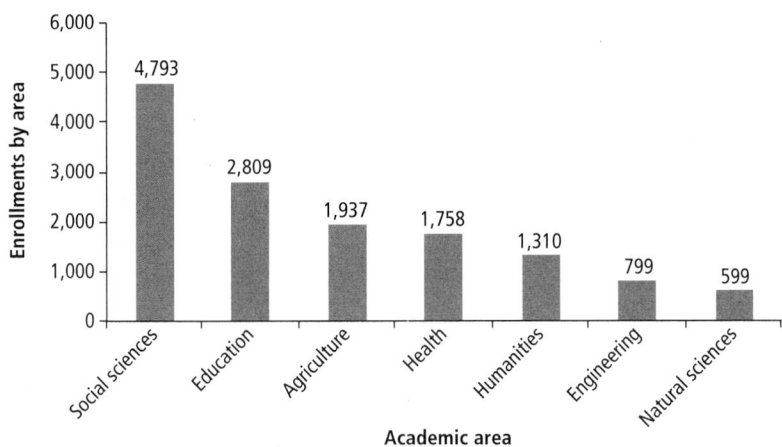

Source: Federal Ministry of Higher Education and Scientific Research.

ALTERNATIVE EDUCATION SYSTEM

The Alternative Education System (AES) integrates a variety of learning programs. AES offers learning opportunities to children and adults who either never attended formal education or have attended school but dropped out and are not likely to reenroll. It offers a variety of learning programs, including some targeted to active and demobilized Sudan People's Liberation Army (SPLA) and other security forces. AES consists of seven main components, often implemented in partnerships with other organizations and with the support of the development partners: Accelerated Learning Programmes (ALPs), Community-based Girls' Schools (CGS), Adult Education, Intensive English Courses (IECs), Interactive Radio Instruction (IRI), Pastoralist Education, and Agro-forestry Education.

Established in 2002, the AES is the second-largest part of the education system. EMIS tallied some 217,239 AES students in 2009 (equivalent to 18 percent of primary school enrollments), while the AES Directorate itself reports as many as 537,108 learners (MoE-AES 2011). Both EMIS and the AES Directorate register some 5,000–6,000 AES teachers. By definition as "alternative," AES enrollments may be harder to assess than enrollments in the formal system. Alternative learning spaces are probably more short-lived, which makes it harder for the MoE to maintain a current list of centers for their annual data collection. Shorter programs may not be in session when the annual education census is carried out, and are not very comparable with longer programs. Also, there may be some double-counting of learners, where dropouts from one program become new entrants in another program.

ALPs account for more than 75 percent of reported AES enrollments. Figure 2.7 provides a breakdown of the 2009 AES enrollment by type of learning program. More than three-quarters of AES students are enrolled in ALPs, which offer an accelerated primary cycle of four years instead of the eight years indicated in the formal system. This program targets older out-of-school children and youth (aged 12–18) but sometimes enrolls children of school age, especially in communities where no primary school facilities are available. One-fifth (19 percent) of AES students attend the classic Adult Literacy Program, while the remaining 3 percent are enrolled in CGS, IECs, and Interactive Radio Instruction. There are no data on enrollments in Pastoralist Education and Agro-forestry Education. This, of course, suggests that AES enrollment data from EMIS are probably underestimated.

Most AES centers do not have their own buildings. In 2009, there were 1,022 AES learning centers, almost half of which were funded by partner agencies (477), according to EMIS. Most AES centers operate within a primary school (50 percent) or some other community structure—such as a church, community building, or secondary school—but more than 20 percent of centers operate "under the tree." The average enrollment per center was 239 students in 2009.

Figure 2.7 AES Enrollments by Type of Program, 2009

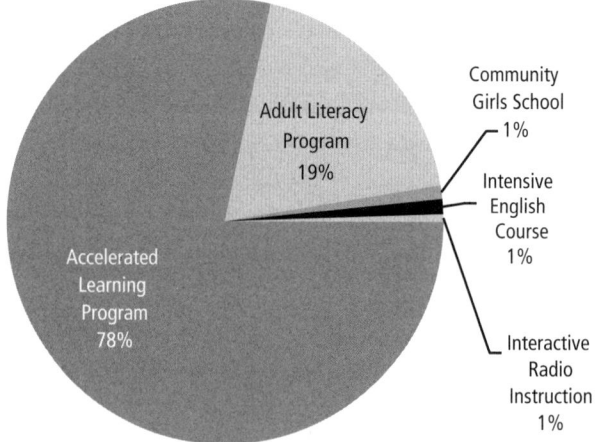

Source: Analysis of EMIS 2009.

KEY FINDINGS

- *Total primary enrollments have risen tremendously over the past decade, expanding the primary school GER from 21 to 72 percent between 2000 and 2009*. This is evidence both of the strong demand for education in South Sudan and of recent years' efforts by GoRSS, private organizations, and communities to expand the network of schools. The majority of primary schools now operate with public funding (85 percent).
- *The expansion of primary schools has not kept up with demand*, however, resulting in many overcrowded schools: the average primary school has 429 students, eight teachers, and three classrooms.
- The secondary school GER is 6 percent based on EMIS data. *Secondary schools appear to have adequate numbers of staff, but lack classrooms and other facilities*. Seventy-five percent of secondary schools are public.
- *Many primary and secondary schools are incomplete*, that is, they do not offer the complete cycle. For primary education, this is a serious barrier for achieving education for all, and at both levels will cause much frustration for citizens who are demanding more schooling for their children.
- In higher education, there are three larger public universities that are funded by the Government of National Unity, as per the CPA. A large proportion of their students attend campuses in northern Sudan, however. There are also a few smaller, private universities in South Sudan. Overall, however, *less than 7,000 students attended university within the borders of the Republic of South Sudan in 2009, while more than 17,000 attended the campuses in the north*.
- *With more than 200,000 students and about 5,000–6,000 teachers, the AES is the second largest part of the education system*. ALPs—which offer a four-year accelerated primary cycle—account for three-quarters of registered AES enrollments. About half of AES learning centers operate within a primary school or some other community structure, but more than 20 percent of centers operate "under the tree."

NOTES

1. Calculated as total enrollment in primary education divided by the population aged 6–13.

2. Many SSA countries have primary GERs that exceed 100 percent due to grade repetition and because several cohorts of children attend school at the same time to catch up after decades of low educational coverage.

3. Using a four-year cohort, the 18- to 21-year-olds, as the reference population.

4. Multishifting helps relieve the burden of overcrowded schools; however, by its nature, it significantly reduces the instructional time each student receives. Evidence shows that there is a close link between instructional time and learning.

CHAPTER 3

Patterns of Student Flow

The patterns of student flow through the cycles of the education system are in a state of transition. The first section of this chapter examines the flow of students through the grades within the formal education system and calculates different indicators of student flow: repetition, intake, completion, and retention rates.[1] Next, the chapter assesses the probability that a child in the Republic of South Sudan has or will access primary schooling. The third section provides data on student flow through the Alternative Education System (AES). The final section looks at the current schooling status of all children and youth and estimates the share who are out of school and overage.

Because several school systems with varying cycle lengths are still operating side by side in South Sudan, the calculation of completion, retention, and transition rates is subject to some caution. When this is a particular concern, the method of calculation has been adapted as indicated in the text.

REPETITION AND SCHOOLING PROFILE IN THE FORMAL SYSTEM

REPETITION

Many students repeat grades in primary schools; in grade 1 in particular, as many as 23 percent could be repeaters. Table 3.1 compares the repetition rates based on two data sources, the Education Management Information System (EMIS) and National Baseline Household Survey (NBHS) data. EMIS reports a level of repetition close to 10 percent in every grade of the primary cycle. The household survey, on the other hand, finds a higher level of repetition overall—15 percent, on average, across the primary cycle, with even higher levels in grade 1 (23 percent) and grade 8 (20 percent).[2]

Table 3.1 Repetition in Primary Schools Based on EMIS and NBHS, 2009

Primary grade	EMIS (%)	NBHS (%)
P1	10	23
P2	10	11
P3	9	11
P4	9	13
P5	9	12
P6	10	12
P7	10	14
P8	11	20
Average primary	10	15

Sources: Analyses of EMIS 2009 and NBHS 2009.

When a student repeats a grade, it places a strain on the education system that must provide and fund an additional year of schooling. There is also evidence that it increases the risk that the student will drop out of school entirely (Glick and Sahn 2010). When parents enroll a child in school, they do so because the expected benefits of schooling exceed the anticipated costs, whether direct cost through fees or parental contributions or opportunity cost. When a child is then asked to repeat a grade, the balance between costs and benefits can easily shift. First, repetition sends a signal to parents that the benefit of educating that child may not be as high as expected. Second, repetition increases the cost to the household of providing that child with the full cycle of education.

SCHOOLING PROFILE

The cross-sectional schooling profile illustrates the extent of access to different parts of the system. Figure 3.1 shows the cross-sectional schooling profile based on EMIS data.[3] In the case of South Sudan, where enrollment rates have expanded rapidly within a few years, the schooling profile is not a good measure of one cohort's flow through the system. Instead, it is simply a picture of the extent of access to different parts of the school system at a single point in time.

The schooling profile for South Sudan shows a system in rapid expansion. Access to the early grades of primary school is far larger than access to upper parts of the system. Rapid expansion of coverage and dropouts explain this pattern. This translates into a primary gross intake rate (GIR)

Figure 3.1 Cross-Sectional Schooling Profiles Based on EMIS, 2009

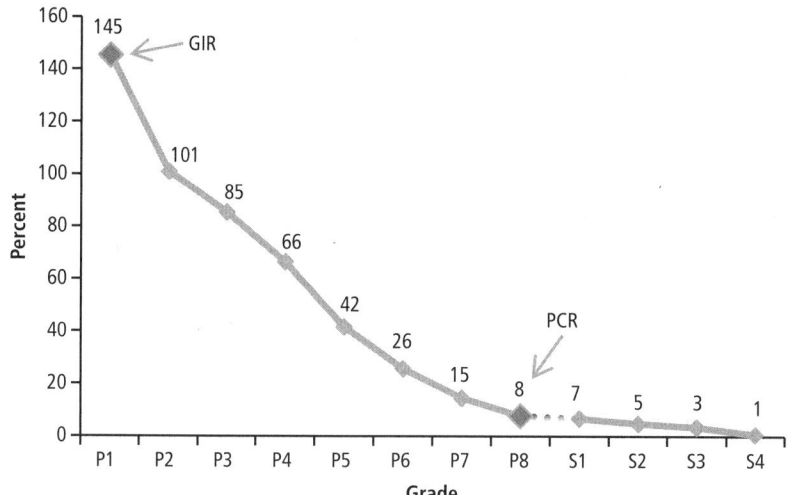

Source: Analysis of EMIS 2009.
Note: The data points of the schooling profiles are calculated as nonrepeaters divided by population of relevant age. GIR = gross intake rate; PCR = primary completion rate.

of 145 percent, a primary-6 completion rate of 26 percent, and a primary-8 completion rate of 8 percent[4] (table 3.2)

With a PCR for grade 6 of 26 percent, there is a very long road ahead to attaining universal primary completion (UPC). The PCR is an important indicator of progress toward UPC, a Millennium Development Goal (MDG). UPC usually refers to completion of a primary cycle of around six years, generally deemed necessary to provide children with basic skills, including lifelong literacy. With a current PCR for the first six years of schooling of 26 percent, South Sudan clearly has a long road ahead to attain UPC.

However, recent progress is well above the average for Sub-Saharan Africa (SSA) countries. Table 3.3 shows the evolution in the gross intake and completion rates in primary education since 2007. The last column

Table 3.2 Gross Intake and Completion Rates, Primary Education, 2009

Rate	EMIS (%)
Gross intake rate	145
Primary completion rate, grade 6	26
Primary completion rate, grade 8	8

Sources: Analyses of EMIS 2009 and NBHS 2009.

Table 3.3   Trend in Gross Intake and Completion Rates, Primary Education, 2009

Rate	2007	2008	2009	Average annual % point gain
Gross intake rate (%)	105	135	145	20.3
PCR, grade 6 (%)	15	21	26	5.2
PCR, grade 8 (%)	6	6	8	1.0

Sources: Analyses of EMIS and population data.

shows the average annual percentage point gain in these indicators: between 2007 and 2009, the GIR gained 20 percentage points per year. The completion rates improved at 5 percentage points per year for grade 6 and 1 percentage point per year for grade 8. The gains in the grade 6 completion rate are quite substantial compared with the average annual gain of 2 percentage points for 33 low-income SSA countries between 1999 and 2009 (Majgaard and Mingat 2012).

Figure 3.2 shows a similar pattern of enrollments by year in higher education. In Juba University, first-year enrollments are 1,200 students, but second-year enrollments are only 600, and third- and fourth-year enrollments are even smaller.

RETENTION

In the case of the Republic of South Sudan, where enrollment rates have expanded rapidly within a few years, the schooling profile is not the best measure of one cohort's flow through the system. The retention rate refers

Figure 3.2   Enrollments at University of Juba, Juba Campus

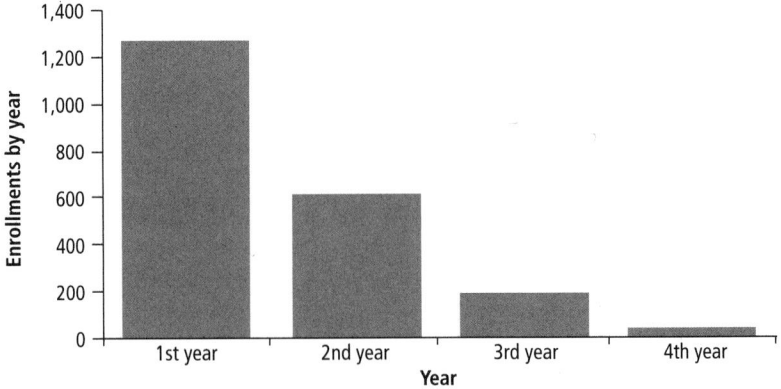

Source: Data collected from Juba University.

to the likelihood of children enrolling in grade 1 still being in school in a later grade. It measures the efficiency of the system to move students through the grades until the end of the cycle in which students have enrolled. Roughly one-third of students are retained until the end of the primary cycle.[5]

Dropout is uneven across the first four grades but steep after grade 4 (figure 3.3). Between grades 1 and 2, the dropout seems large with only 73 percent of those initially enrolled apparently still in school by grade 2. Once in grade 2, however, most pupils remain in school until grade 4. After grade 4, the dropout is steep again with, on average, 13 percent of those initially enrolled dropping out every year.

SKIPPING GRADES

Surprisingly, according to NBHS, 21 percent of those enrolled in 2009 reported having skipped the previous grade (table 3.4). This is another indication of the fluidity of the school system in South Sudan. The pattern shows poor student flow management and, more generally, poor knowledge of the actual level of student learning and curricula.

COHORT ACCESS AND MULTICOHORT EFFECTS

Figure 3.4 shows the likelihood, by age, that children and youth have ever been enrolled in primary schooling. The likelihood of "ever" being

Figure 3.3 Retention Profile Based on EMIS, 2009

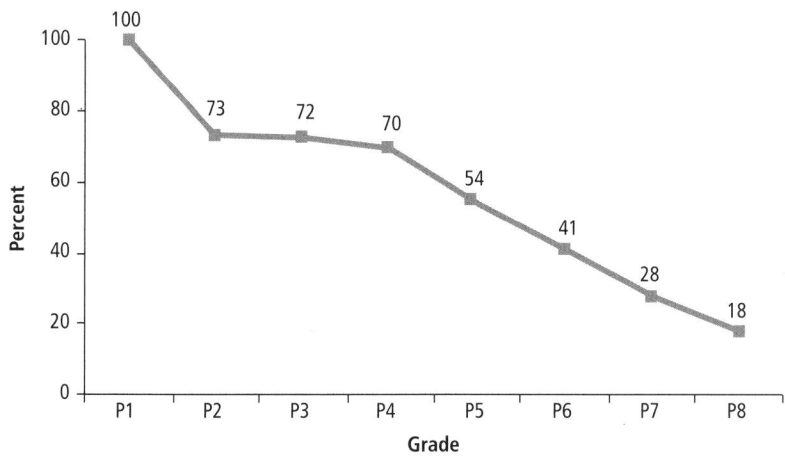

Source: Last column of table D.2 (appendix D).

Table 3.4   Students Skipping Grades, 2009

Grade skipped	Students skipping grade	As share of enrollments in grade (%)
Skipping grade 1	43,485	16
Skipping grade 2	54,505	22
Skipping grade 3	38,803	21
Skipping grade 4	33,238	25
Skipping grade 5	24,133	24
Skipping grade 6	19,777	26
Skipping grade 7	14,354	23
Overall	228,295	21

Source: Analysis of NBHS 2009.

Figure 3.4   Probability of Ever Enrolling in Primary Schooling, 2009

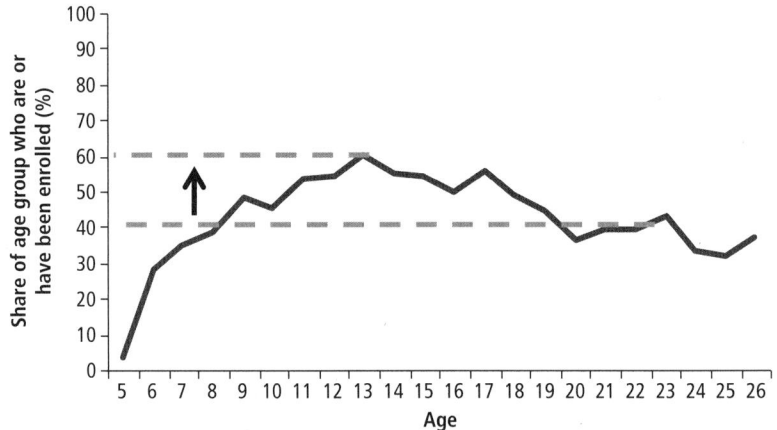

Source: Analysis of NBHS 2009.

enrolled in primary school increases consistently until reaching a peak at age 13. At age 13, 60 percent of the population reports having been enrolled in primary school. This peak value is also known as the *cohort access rate*, as it expresses the proportion of the children that ever access education as current enrollment rates.

Access to primary schooling has improved from 40 to 60 percent of a cohort over 10 years. Figure 3.4 indicates that only about 40 percent of 23-year-olds report ever having been enrolled in school.

Finally, figure 3.4 provides information about the ages at which children enter school. The peak at age 13 indicates that children enter school at all ages between 5 and 13, but that if they are not enrolled by age 13, it is unlikely that they will ever enroll.

There is a wide gap between the gross intake rate of 124 percent reported above and the cohort access rate of 60 percent. This results from the presence of children from different age cohorts accessing school at the same time—common in rapidly expanding school systems, such as when new schools are opened where there were none before or when school fees are eliminated.[6]

STUDENT FLOW IN THE ALTERNATIVE EDUCATION SYSTEM

The profile of enrollments and nonrepeaters in AES, shown in figure 3.5, shows declining enrollments with increasing grade, except for grade 4.[7] Since AES by its very nature has a flexible design, this could indicate that there are several entry points to the cycle. Among the reasons given for dropout—as reported by EMIS—family responsibilities were by far the most common, outranking dropout resulting from work, health conditions, or fees. Repetition in AES is 13 percent across all grades, but highest in the three first grades.

CURRENT SCHOOLING STATUS OF ALL CHILDREN AND YOUTH

More than half of school-age children and youth are out of school. While the data presented in this chapter so far include only those enrolled, figure 3.6 indicates the schooling status of all children and youth between

Figure 3.5   Enrollments and Nonrepeaters by Grade in AES, 2009

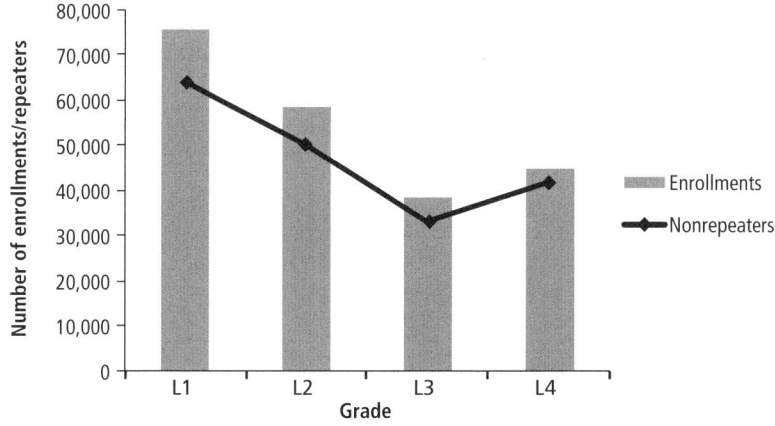

Source: Analysis of EMIS 2009.

Figure 3.6   Schooling Status by Age, 2009

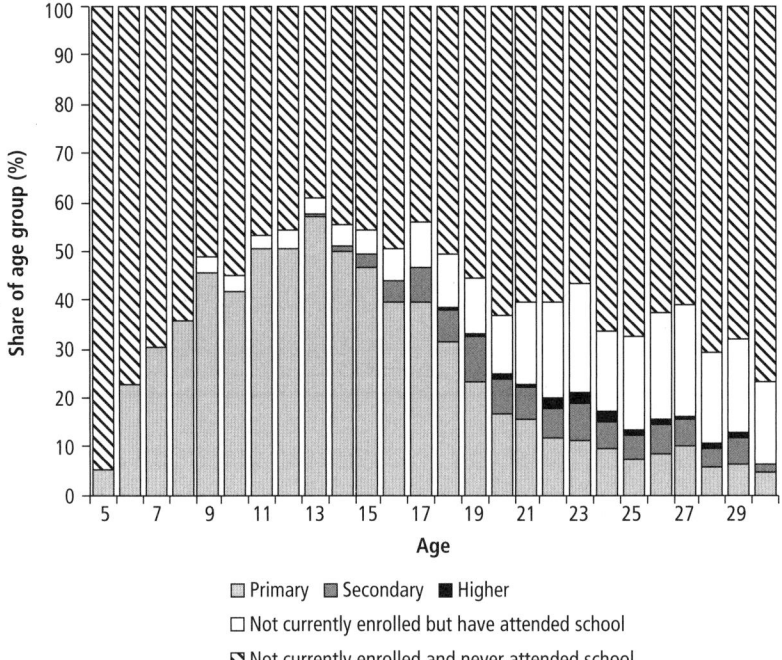

Source: Analysis of NBHS 2009.

the ages of 5 and 30. For those enrolled in school, the chart shows what level that they are enrolled in; for those out of school, it shows whether they have ever been enrolled. Clearly, most are out of school *and* have never been to school.

The education system is in a catch-up phase, dealing with many cohorts of youth that had little access to schooling. Figure 3.6 also illustrates that overage enrollment is a widespread feature of the education system. This is seen both by the low enrollment of, in particular, the 6- to 8-year-olds, and by the continued enrollment of youth in their 20s in both primary and secondary schools. Dealing with such diversity in the schools is a challenge. Although this will be a feature of the system for the next several years, over time it will probably self-correct as children start enrolling closer to the official age and the "multicohort" effect diminishes. As shown in table 3.5, across the primary cycle, 44 percent of students are five or more years overage for the grade they are attending. The share is highest in the upper grades.

With so many children still out of formal schooling, nonformal options will be needed for many years to come. Chapter 4 presents addi-

Table 3.5 Share of Primary School Pupils Five or More Years Overage for Their Grade, 2009

Grade	Share of pupils five or more years overage (%)
P1	21 (11 years or older)
P2	39 (12 or older)
P3	47 (13 or older)
P4	54 (14 or older)
P5	56 (15 or older)
P6	60 (16 or older)
P7	62 (17 or older)
P8	66 (18 or older)
P1–P8	44

Source: Analysis of NBHS 2009.

tional data on both out-of-school children of primary school-age and the older nonliterate children and youth.

KEY FINDINGS

- *After decades of low educational access, the Republic of South Sudan's system is in a catch-up phase.* This is reflected in the very high value of the GIR to primary education: at 145 percent in 2009, this indicator is inflated by the multiple cohorts entering schools at the same time.
- *In the past two years, the PCR, corresponding to six years of primary education, improved by about 5 percentage points per year,* from 15 percent in 2007 to 26 percent in 2009. The average improvement for 33 low-income SSA countries was 2 percentage points per year.
- *Many children remain out of school.* Only 60 percent of children in their early teens report ever having been enrolled in school. However, this is much higher than 10 years ago, when only 40 percent of the same age group had ever enrolled.
- *Only about a third of those who enroll in primary school reach the end of the primary cycle.* Retention is fairly good until grade 4, but after grade 4, dropout is steep and persistent. The primary completion rate is 24 percent for six years of primary school and only 8 percent for the whole eight-year cycle.
- *The education system is affected by high repetition (15 percent of those enrolled are repeaters), a considerable number of students skipping*

grades, and an extraordinarily large number of overage students. Some of these aspects are likely transitional and will ease over time, as the system stabilizes. This is the case for the overage students, for example. Other aspects are more at risk of becoming permanent features of the education system, such as the high repetition and dropout rates.

NOTES

1. Because several school systems with varying cycle lengths are still operating side by side in South Sudan, the calculation of certain student flow indicators is messy. This affects mostly the calculation of the completion, retention, and transition rates. When this is a particular concern, the method of calculation has been adapted as indicated in the text.

2. The data for secondary education are not yet reliable enough to calculate repetition rates.

3. Each data point in the schooling profile corresponds to an "access rate" to that grade, which is calculated as the nonrepeaters in the grade (that is, enrollments net of repeaters) divided by the population of relevant age for the grade. The first data point is equivalent to the primary gross intake rate (GIR), while the P8 data point is equivalent to the primary completion rate (PCR).

4. Appendix D presents how EMIS data may be combined with the NBHS repetition structure to produce an adjusted schooling profile, which gives a gross intake rate of 124 percent and a primary-8 completion rate of 7 percent.

5. Appendix D describes the methodology for calculating the retention rate.

6. See, for example, Avenstrup, Liang, and Nellemann (2004) for a description of the surges in enrollments in Kenya, Lesotho, Malawi, and Uganda, when school fees were eliminated.

7. With only one year of EMIS data for AES and no household survey data to provide an added perspective, limited analysis can be done of the student flow through AES.

CHAPTER 4

Disparities in School Participation

A ccess to education has always been very inequitable in the Republic of South Sudan, resulting in wide disparities in literacy rates across gender and across the 10 states (as shown in chapter 1). Although gaps in access to primary school are diminishing as more and more children become enrolled, disparities still affect all levels of education. The chapter first explores the disparities between girls and boys, rural and urban, and poor and rich children. Next, it looks at disparities across states. Finally, it presents figures on the number and characteristics of out-of-school and nonliterate youth.

SOCIOECONOMIC DISPARITIES

SOCIOECONOMIC DISPARITIES IN PRIMARY SCHOOL

There are wide disparities in the chances that a child will ever enroll in primary school, depending on whether the child is urban or rural, rich or poor, or boy or girl. As shown in figure 4.1, the widest disparities are associated with the urban-rural and rich-poor dimensions, but there are also strong gender disparities. Thus, urban children are 33 percentage points more likely to ever enroll in grade 1 than rural children. Children from the richest quintile are 32 percentage points more likely to enroll in grade 1 than children from the poorest quintile. And boys are 13 percentage points more likely to ever enroll in grade 1 than girls.

There are almost equally wide socioeconomic disparities in the retention rate to the last grade of primary school. For those children who did enroll in school, the gaps in the likelihood of still being in school by the last grade are again widest for the urban-rural and rich-poor dimensions. Urban children are 27 percentage points more likely than rural children

Figure 4.1 Disparities in Access to and Retention in Primary Education, 2009

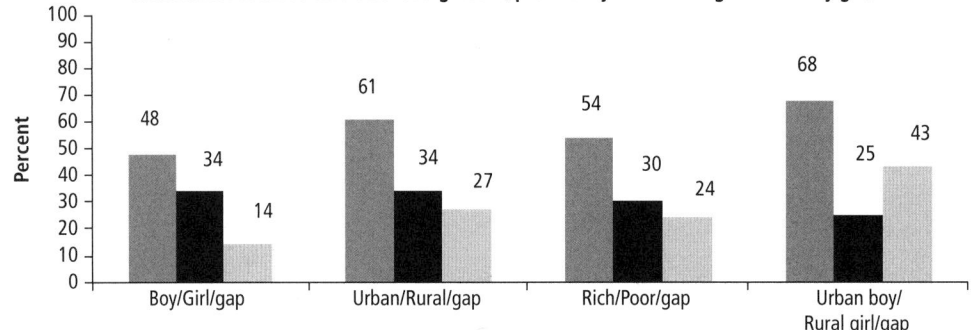

Source: Analysis of NBHS 2009.
Note: The analysis of access to grade 1 is based on children ages 11–17, while the analysis of retention to grade 8 is based on youth ages 19–27. "Rich" refers to the 20 percent richest and "poor" to the 20 percent poorest in the population.

to still be in school by grade 8, children from the richest quintile are 24 percentage points more likely to still be in school than children from the poorest quintile, and boys are 14 percentage points more likely than girls to remain enrolled until grade 8.

As figure 4.1 shows, rural girls are much less likely than urban boys to ever enroll in school. Girls living in rural areas are facing very difficult odds: their chance of ever enrolling in school is only 42 percent compared with 86 percent for urban boys.

Even when enrolled, rural girls are also much less likely than urban boys to complete the primary cycle. The retention of rural girls to the last grade of the primary cycle is only 24 percent (compared with 68 percent for urban boys, resulting in a gap of 43 percentage points). We would see even higher gaps if these two groups, rural girls and urban boys, were further disaggregated by, for example, income, state, ethnic group, or nomadic population.[1] Reaching the Millennium Development Goal (MDG) of universal primary completion (UPC) will require a concerted effort to close all these gaps.

DISPARITIES IN REASONS FOR NOT ATTENDING SCHOOL

When asked why their children were not in school, parents gave similar reasons for their sons as for their daughters, according to the National Baseline Household Survey (NBHS) (figure 4.2): "no money for school costs" and "school too far from home." This is a major change from 2001, when parents reported different reasons for girls and boys not in school. According to a Care International survey of schools,[2] girls' nonattendance was attributed to domestic chores while boys' was attributed to distance to school. This could indicate either that there has been a change in attitudes toward girls' school participation or that out-of-school girls and boys now have more similar characteristics than a decade ago, as the gender gap in access to schooling is narrowing.

Urban and rural children report different reasons for nonattendance. For rural families, the main reason given for children's nonattendance is "school too far from home," at 24 percent. Distance to school is only an issue for 9 percent of urban families. This indicates the presence of considerable supply-side issues in rural areas, where many children may not have a school that is close enough for them to attend. Simply building more schools may be enough to bring many additional children into

Figure 4.2 Reasons for Not Attending School, Boys and Girls, Urban and Rural, 2009

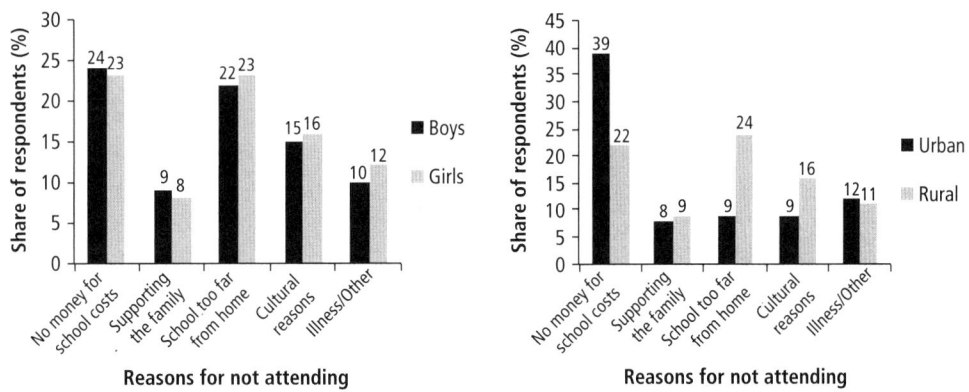

Source: Analysis of NBHS 2009.
Note: Based on children ages 6–15 who were not attending school at the time. In the survey, parents were able to indicate either one or several reasons for nonattendance, so the five reasons are not mutually exclusive.

classrooms. The main reason for nonattendance in urban areas is "no money for school costs," reported by as many as 39 percent of urban families, while only 22 percent of rural residents give this reason. This difference may be a result of urban schools charging higher fees than rural schools, as some of the collected information would indicate.[3]

GENDER DISPARITIES ACROSS ALL LEVELS OF EDUCATION

Clearly, disadvantages to girls' school participation affect all levels of education, although the gender gap is wider in secondary and higher education than in primary. The Alternative Education System (AES) has the least gender bias of all. Based on 2009 enrollment data from the Education Management Information System (EMIS), girls made up 37 percent of total enrollments in primary schools, 27 percent in secondary schools, and 24 percent in higher education (the female enrollment share is only about 20 percent on South Sudan's campuses).[4] Further, girls made up 42 percent of enrollments in AES and 24 percent of enrollments at teacher training institutes (TTIs) (figure 4.3).

Because the system is in a catch-up phase with children from many different age groups enrolling in school at the same time, analyzing total current enrollment does not give an accurate picture of the gender gap between different generations. In fact, the gender gap in primary education and literacy has been diminishing at an impressive rate over the past two decades. Using household survey data comparing the share of girls

Figure 4.3   Female Share by Level of Education Based on EMIS Data, 2009

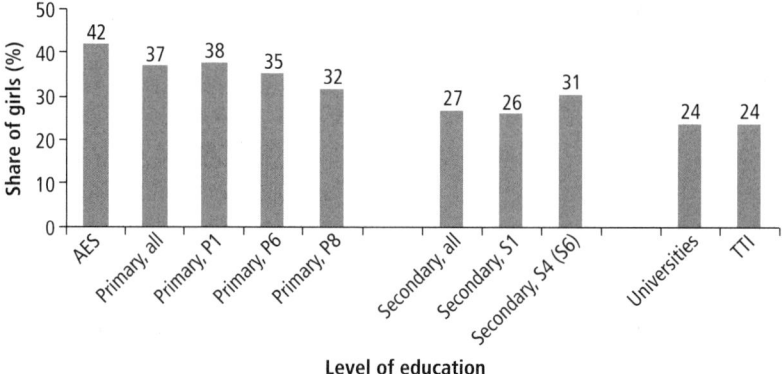

Source: Analysis of EMIS 2009.
Note: Data for universities include enrollments on Khartoum campuses, but exclude enrollments on Juba University's Juba campus for lack of gender-disaggregated data.
AES = Alternative Education System; TTI = Teacher Training Institute.

Figure 4.4 Female Share by Educational Attainment and in Literate Population, 2009

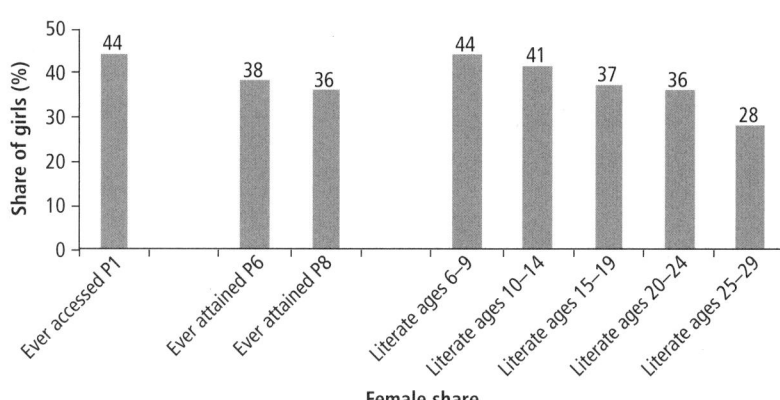

Source: Analysis of NBHS 2009.
Note: This analysis assumes that the female share of the population is 50 percent in the age groups shown. Analysis of access is based on children aged 11–17, while analysis of attainment of grade 6 or 8 is based on youth aged 19–27.

that have ever enrolled in school or ever attained P6 or P8 (but may not currently be enrolled), figure 4.4 indicates that the share of girls is several percentage points higher than in figure 4.3. For an added perspective, figure 4.4 also provides the female share of literate individuals in different age groups, showing a considerable increase in the female share of the literate population across the five age groups, from 28 percent for women 25–29 years old to 44 percent for girls 6–9 years old. If this trend continues, the gap between girls and boys in terms of primary schooling and literacy is set to close within a relatively short period of time.

Girls also have higher repetition rates across different levels of education. According to EMIS 2009, repetition rates were 11 percent for girls and 9 percent for boys in primary school; 9 percent for girls and 6 percent for boys in secondary school; and 15 percent for girls and 12 percent for boys in AES.

REGIONAL DISPARITIES

REGIONAL DISPARITIES IN THE PRIMARY SCHOOL ENROLLMENT

There are wide disparities in the primary school gross enrollment rate (GER) across states. This is shown in figure 4.5, which divides the 10 states into three groups based on the level of their GER:

- *States with relatively high primary school enrollment.* These states include Western Equatoria, Upper Nile, and Central Equatoria, all with a primary

Figure 4.5 Disparities in Primary School GER across States, 2009

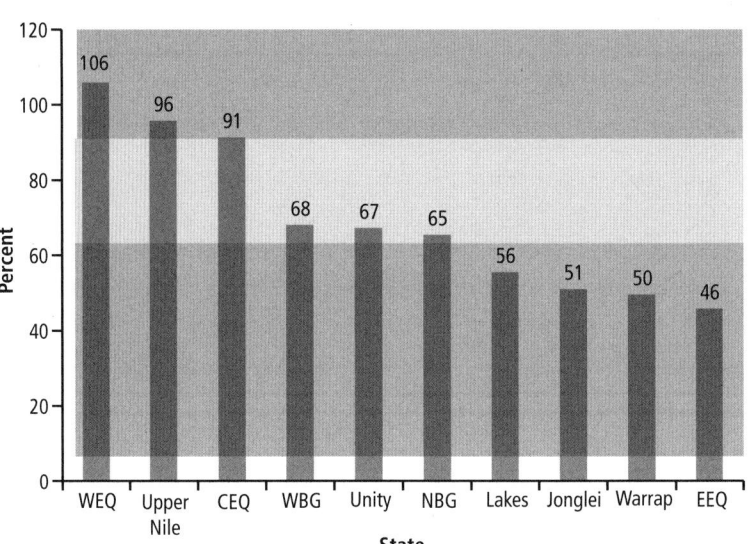

Source: Analysis of NBHS 2009.
Note: See appendix D for a comparison of states' primary school GER based on EMIS and NBHS.
CEQ = Central Equatoria; EEQ = Eastern Equatoria; NBG = Northern Bahr Ghazal; WBG = Western Bahr Ghazal; WEQ = Western Equatoria.

school GER above 90 percent. Upper Nile historically has had a more developed education system and is the state with the highest adult literacy rate in South Sudan.[5] Central Equatoria is the capital region and as such would be expected to have above-average school enrollment.

- *States with average primary school enrollment.* Three states fall into this category, all with a primary school GER between 60 and 90 percent: Western Bahr Ghazal, Unity, and Northern Bahr Ghazal.
- *States with relatively low primary school enrollment.* This group comprises four states with primary school GER below 60 percent: Lakes, Jonglei, Warrap, and Eastern Equatoria. The same four states have the lowest adult literacy rates in South Sudan, all in the 15–19 percent range, compared with 27 percent for the country as a whole. These states will need further support in terms of expanding their education systems.

REGIONAL DISPARITIES IN PRIMARY SCHOOL ENTRY AND ATTAINMENT

Table 4.1 analyzes the disparities across states in the rates of entry to grade 1 and attainment of grade 8 based on household survey data.[6] Universal primary completion (UPC) can be achieved only if all children both enroll in school (grade 1) and complete a full course of primary school-

Table 4.1 Disparities in Primary School Entry, Attainment, and Retention Rates across States and by Gender, 2009

States listed in order of descending primary GER	Probability of ever entering P1 (cohort access rate)			Probability of attaining P8 (cohort completion rate)			Retention
	All	Girls	Gender gap (% point)	All	Girls	Gender gap (% point)	All
High enrollment states							
Western Equatoria	86	81	8	25	17	15	29
Upper Nile	77	72	11	36	25	19	47
Central Equatoria	71	65	13	43	32	20	60
Average three states	78	73	11	35	25	18	45
Average enrollment states							
Western Bahr el Ghazal	55	47	15	28	18	17	50
Unity	55	48	15	20	12	13	36
Northern Bahr el Ghazal	54	47	15	19	11	14	36
Average three states	55	47	15	22	14	15	41
Low enrollment states							
Lakes	41	34	15	15	8	11	36
Jonglei	40	32	15	11	6	9	27
Warrap	35	27	14	11	6	9	31
Eastern Equatoria	37	29	15	20	13	14	54
Average four states	38	31	15	14	8	11	37
Average all	**55**	**48**	**13**	**24**	**17**	**13**	**43**

Source: Analysis of NBHS 2009.

ing. Therefore, analyzing entry and attainment rates allows us to distinguish between states that have problems with securing access to grade 1, retention within the cycle, or both.

At 43 percent, Central Equatoria has the highest P8 attainment rate of all the states. The states are listed in order of ascending primary GER, but the table shows that states with higher GER do not always have higher entry and attainment rates. In terms of attainment of the primary cycle—the main indicators of progress toward UPC—Central Equatoria is ahead of all other states, including the other two high-enrollment states, although they have a higher GER. This is a result of Central Equatoria having the best retention within the primary cycle out of all the states, at 60 percent compared with an average of 43 percent for South Sudan as a whole.

None of the states are close to 100 percent in either entry or attainment. But some states have much more work ahead of them than others and will need more support to attain these goals. The table also provides the size of the gender gap, in percentage points, at the points of entry and exit of the primary cycle. Altogether, the data provided in table 4.1 give a helpful snapshot of each state's progress toward and distance from UPC. Upon entry, the gender gap is narrowest in the states with the highest enrollment, while the pattern is reversed upon exit, where the high enrollment states have surprisingly large gaps between girls' and boys' attainment. For additional comparative information on enrollment patterns in the states, appendix F presents the educational pyramids of each state.

OUT-OF-SCHOOL CHILDREN

Figure 4.6 displays the current enrollment status of children and youth in urban and rural areas, respectively. The two panels show the proportion of each single age group that is enrolled in primary, secondary, and higher education. Clearly, children in urban areas are much more likely to be enrolled in any level of education than rural children. For this reason, and because most of the population live in rural areas, most out-of-school children are rural. Out of school, in this report, is understood to mean primary school-age children who are not attending school (neither primary, nor secondary or higher education).

To estimate the number of out-of-school children, we focus on the 8- to 15-year-olds, an eight-year cohort that approximates better when South Sudan's children are normally in school than the official 6–13 age group.[7] In this age group, 27 percent are out of school in urban areas compared to 58 percent in rural areas, for a South Sudan average of 53 percent of 8- to 15-year-olds. In absolute numbers, this means that 1 million children

Figure 4.6 Youth Cohorts by Level of Schooling in Urban and Rural Areas, 2009

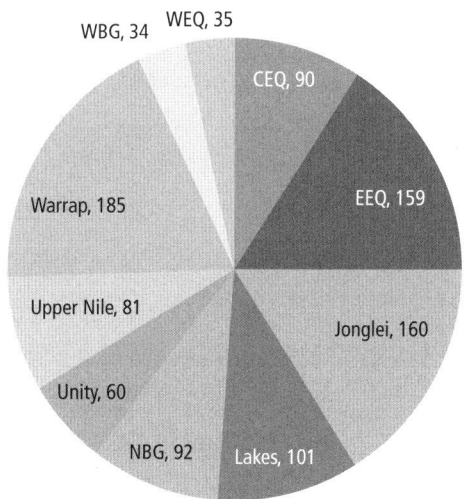

Source: Analysis of the 2009 NBHS.

are out of (primary) school in South Sudan. Urban areas are home to an estimated 75,000 out-of-school children, while almost 925,000 out-of-school children live in rural areas. Most of the out-of-school children live in Warrap, Jonglei, or Eastern Equatoria, as shown in figure 4.7.

Figure 4.7 Out-of-School Children by State (Thousands), 2009

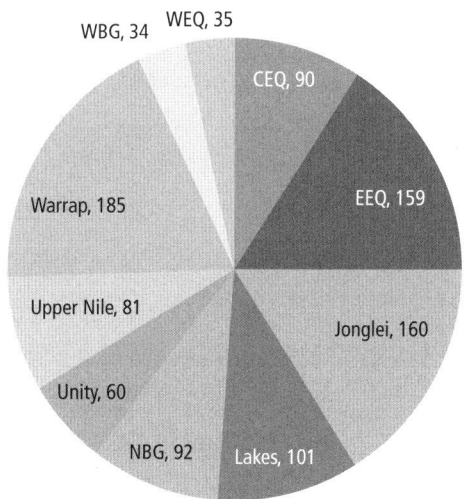

Source: Analysis of NBHS 2009.
Note: Includes children ages 8–15 who are not enrolled in any level. CEQ = Central Equatoria; EEQ = Eastern Equatoria; NBG = Northern Bahr Ghazal; WBG = Western Bahr Ghazal; WEQ = Western Equatoria.

NONLITERATE YOUTH AND AES

Within the 15–40 age group, an estimated 2.2 million are nonliterate out of a total population[8] of about 3.2 million ages 15–40. Paradoxically, although literacy rates have improved over time, most nonliterates are young because of South Sudan's strong population growth, as illustrated in figure 4.8.

For comparison, AES enrolls approximately 170,000 students in the 15–40 age group. Since most are enrolled in multiyear AES programs, such as the four-year Accelerated Learning Programme (ALP), the output of graduating students is likely below 50,000 a year. Thus, of the "stock" of 2.2 million nonliterate, only about 50,000 individuals exit every year ("flow").

Given that 65 percent or almost two-thirds of nonliterate youth are female, strictly speaking, gender equity in AES would require that 65 percent of AES enrollments are female. Since the share is currently only 42 percent, this points to the need for better targeting of AES services to girls and women. Currently, only in Upper Nile and Western Equatoria are more women enrolled in AES than men.

Nonliterate individuals are most likely to live in Warrap or Jonglei. The left panel of figure 4.9 shows the breakdown, by state, of the nonliterate population. Warrap and Jonglei account for the largest shares, 18 percent and 16 percent, respectively, of this group. The right panel shows the breakdown of AES enrollments by state. Most AES enrollments are in Unity and Northern Bahr Ghazal, but there are also many in Jonglei. Comparing the two panels may give an indication of where more AES centers are needed. Warrap stands out as having only 2 percent of all AES

Figure 4.8 Population, Ages 15–40, by Gender and Literacy Status, 2009

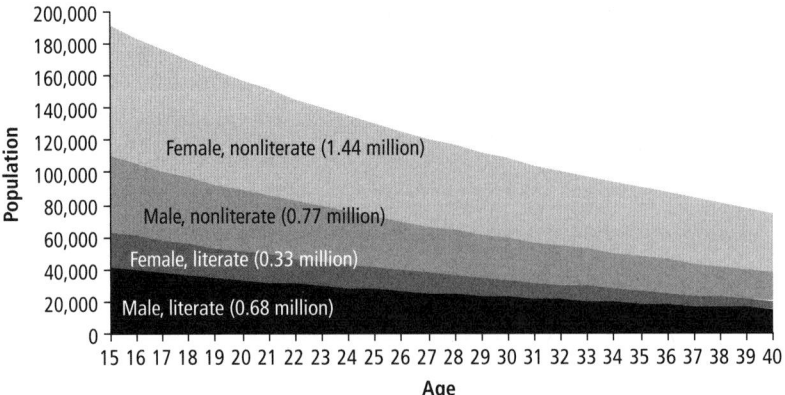

Source: Analysis of NBHS 2009.
Note: Data across ages were smoothed for clarity.

Figure 4.9 Comparison of Nonliterate Population and AES Enrollments, by State Where They Live, 2009

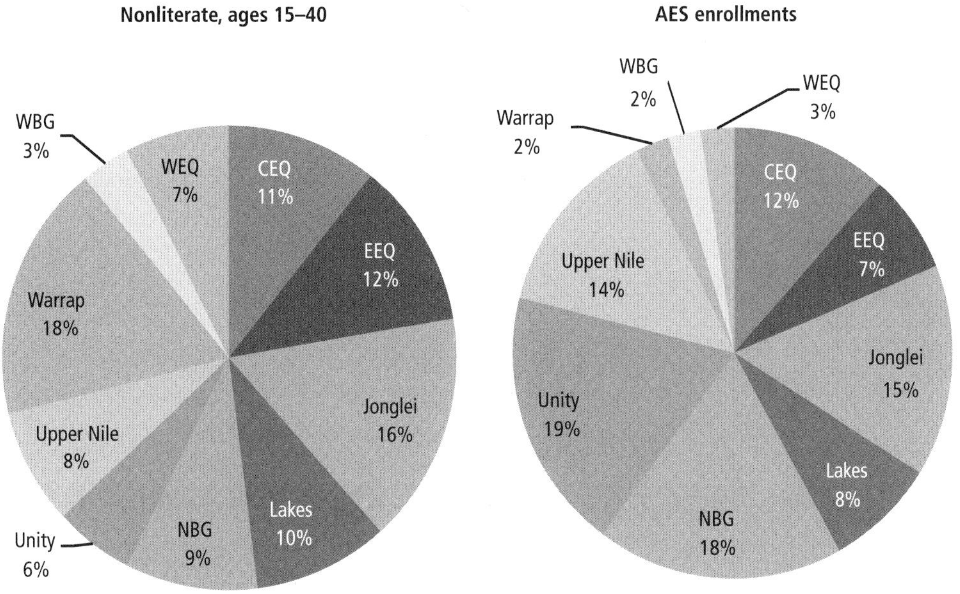

Nonliterate, ages 15–40

AES enrollments

Sources: Data on nonliterate population are based on NBHS 2009. Data on AES enrollments are based on EMIS 2009.
CEQ = Central Equatoria; EEQ = Eastern Equatoria; NBG = Northern Bahr Ghazal; WBG = Western Bahr Ghazal; WEQ = Western Equatoria.

enrollments, while it accounts for as much as 18 percent of the nonliterate target group. There also seems to be a deficit of AES services in Eastern Equatoria, which is home to 12 percent of the nonliterate target population but only 7 percent of AES enrollments.

KEY FINDINGS

- The likelihood that children from different population groups ever enroll in grade 1 and remain in school until grade 8 depends on various socioeconomic factors. *Rural children, poorer children, and girls are all at a considerable disadvantage*, with the widest gaps associated with the urban-rural and rich-poor dimensions.

- *While there continues to be a gap between boys' and girls' enrollment at all levels of education, it has diminished greatly over recent years*. The gender gap is much smaller for the current generation of children than among adults, even among young adults under age 30. This shows that girls are among the main beneficiaries of the recent expansion in educational coverage. Gaps in school participation remain, however, and girls are also affected by higher repetition and dropout rates than boys.

- *Overall, the two most important reasons provided for nonattendance are cost of schooling and distance to school.* Boys and girls provide largely the same reasons for not being in school. But for urban children, the main reason for nonattendance is the cost of schooling; for rural children, the main reason provided is distance to school.

- *The 10 states can be categorized into three groups with widely different primary school GERs.* Three states have gross enrollment rates of around 95–100 percent, another three states have gross enrollment rates around 65–70 percent, and four states have gross enrollment rates around 50 percent. This indicator seems to correlate with the states' literacy rates, indicating that states that historically had less-developed education systems are still behind. These states may need further support to catch up with the rest, so inequities of the past do not become permanent features of the education system.

- *Central Equatoria has the highest rate of P8 attainment, at 43 percent, and Jonglei and Warrap have the lowest, at 11 percent; but none of the states are close to 100 percent in either entry or attainment at the primary level.* Consequently, all states need to work at improving both access to grade 1 and retention within the primary cycle, with some needing more support to attain these goals (see table 4.1).

- *Currently, South Sudan has an estimated 1 million out-of-school children,* that is, children who should be in primary school but are not. About 75,000 of these live in urban areas and 925,000 in rural areas, most likely in Warrap, Jonglei, or Eastern Equatoria.

- *An estimated 2.2 million population of South Sudan in the 15–40 age group are nonliterate and could benefit from literacy training.* Although literacy rates have improved over time, most nonliterate individuals are at the younger end of this range because of South Sudan's strong population growth and young population.

NOTES

1. This was not done because of lack of information on some of these dimensions in the household survey, NBHS, on which this analysis is based, and because the sample size does not allow for much disaggregation.

2. Reported in MoEST/UNICEF (2008).

3. The director general of one state indicated that fees were higher in urban than in rural schools (NBHS, October 2009).

4. This figure excludes enrollments at Juba University, Juba campus, for lack of data. At Juba University in Khartoum, the female enrollment share is 22 percent.

5. Adult literacy rates by state are provided in chapter 1. Upper Nile ranks highest with a rate of 45 percent, compared with the Republic of South Sudan's average of 27 percent.

6. Household survey data seem to be the better choice for state-level analyses because EMIS (combined with population) data produce primary education coverage indicators that are counterintuitive for some states and underestimate secondary school coverage.

7. We did not use the official age for primary, 6–13, because with so many children enrolling late, a 6- or 7-year-old who is not enrolled in the Republic of South Sudan cannot really be considered out of school, but rather not in school yet. The 8- to 15-year-old age group has a much higher rate of school participation than the 6- to 13-year-old age group.

8. These figures are based on the NBHS and may not be entirely consistent with the population census figures.

CHAPTER 5

Student Learning and Service Delivery

An uncontested mandate of the education sector is to build knowledge and skills in the school population. Fulfillment of this mandate is directly dependent on the quality of services offered in schools and classrooms. Effective service delivery is associated with the promotion of students from grade to grade, completion of primary and secondary education, and proficiency in learning. Delivering quality education across the Republic of South Sudan will be a key challenge, compounded by its status as a new country. This chapter examines aspects of student achievement and service delivery in South Sudanese schools, with the main focus being on primary education.

DATA SOURCES

The main source of data for this chapter is the Ministry of Education (MoE) Service Delivery Study (SDS), a survey of a sample of 107 primary schools across four states: Central Equatoria, Lakes, Upper Nile, and Western Bahr Gazal. The four states were selected to represent South Sudan's major regions. The Service Delivery Study included questionnaires on schooling conditions, classroom observation, and student assessment tests in language and mathematics of 1,800 grade 6 students. Data collection took place in July and August 2010. Appendix A provides more information about the study.

STUDENT LEARNING OUTCOMES IN PRIMARY EDUCATION

There are two ways a school system can monitor and evaluate levels of student achievement: through examinations or learning assessments. Examinations are aligned with the school curriculum and test students on their curricular knowledge. They consequently certify a student's readiness to enter the next grade or level of instruction. Learning assessments, on the other hand, test standard skills of students on a sample basis. If conducted annually or every two to three years, student assessments allow for comparisons over time. In addition, the results reflect the effectiveness of institutions to deliver quality services.

STUDENT EXAMINATION RESULTS

Each state in South Sudan has its own system of examinations in primary education. Success in the grade 8 exam certifies students and allows them to proceed to secondary school. Independent units in each state are responsible for developing and conducting the state's grade 8 final exam. Normally, the number of students appearing for the exam would be a proportion of students in grade 8. However, in South Sudan the total number of students registering (39,315) far exceeded the number in grade 8 in 2009 (18,295). This indicates that many students from the Alternative Education System (AES)—which in 2009 enrolled more than 40,000 in its last grade—sit for the exam to obtain primary school certification.

Though it is not possible to compare student performance across South Sudan and over time, table 5.1 captures the success rate of students in each state. Overall, about 80 percent of the registered students were successful in the grade 8 exams. Pass rates for boys ranged from 62 per-

Table 5.1 Student Performance in Grade 8 Examinations, 2009

State	% Boys passed	% Girls passed
Central Equatoria	72	62
Eastern Equatoria	71	59
Jonglei	62	80
Lakes	92	82
Northern Bahr Ghazal	83	82
Unity	86	94
Upper Nile	87	85
Warrap	91	88
Western Bahr Ghazal	82	82
Western Equatoria	80	83
Total for the Republic of South Sudan	81	80

Source: Analysis of EMIS 2009.

cent in Jonglei to 92 percent in Lakes and pass rates for girls ranged from 59 percent in Eastern Equatoria to 94 percent in Unity. In three states (Central and Eastern Equatoria, and Lakes), girls performed much worse than boys, and in two states (Jonglei and Unity), this situation was reversed.

STUDENT ASSESSMENT RESULTS

The Service Delivery Study included learning assessments in mathematics and language and a student background questionnaire. The mathematics test consisted of 30 test items from the 1995 or 2003 Trends in International Mathematics and Science Study (TIMSS) fourth-grade assessment and the language test of 25 items from the 1995 or 2001 Progress in International Reading Literacy Study (PIRLS) fourth-grade assessment. Taking into account the years lost due to the conflict in South Sudan, the research team decided to administer the test to students in grade 6 instead of grade 4.[1] Of the students who took the test, only 3 percent were in the correct age group for grade 6 (11 years old), 45 percent were in the 12–16 age group, and the remaining students were more than 16 years old.

The overall performance of students in South Sudan is weak in both mathematics and language. The mean score for the four states in mathematics is 29 percent and in language 35 percent. In figure 5.1, the distribution of test scores in both subjects skews to the left, pointing to the small share of students that was able to answer most of the questions correctly. In mathematics, less than 8 percent of students scored 50 percent and above, and less than 1 percent scored above 75 percent. For language,

Figure 5.1 Distribution of Test Scores for Grade 6 Students in Mathematics and Language, 2009

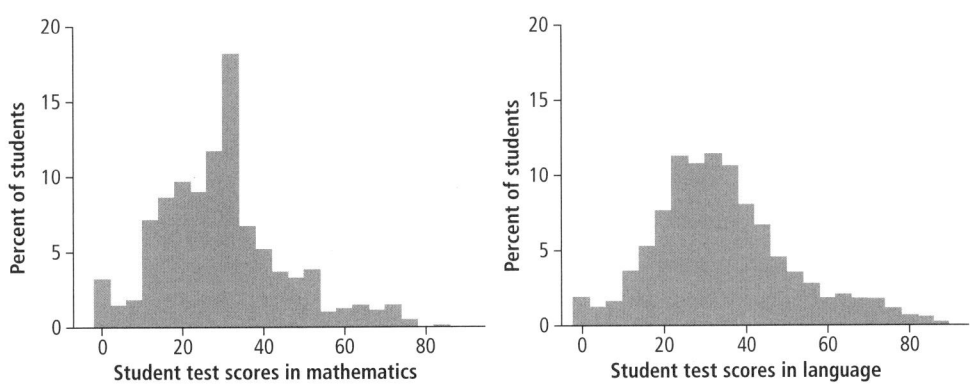

Source: Analysis of SDS 2010.
Note: Each chart shows a histogram of the test scores.

this number is 16 percent and 4 percent, respectively. To give an idea of the international range of results, both tests consisted of a series of multiple choice questions, each with four options, so a randomly completed test questionnaire would give an average score of around 25 percent. Fourth-graders in Singaporean schools score around 80 percent on similar tests (more international comparisons are shown later).

Student performance in Lakes state is higher in both mathematics and language compared to the other three states (table 5.2). In mathematics, the average student answered 40 percent of the questions correctly compared to Central Equatoria with 27 percent, Upper Nile with 21 percent, and Western Bahr Ghazal with 28 percent. Similarly, in language, the average student score is 47 percent; again, the Lakes state score is the highest (47 percent) compared to Central Equatoria with 33 percent, Upper Nile with 24 percent, and Western Bahr Ghazal with 32 percent.

The box plots (figure 5.2) display the wide variation in school-level average scores. Although Lakes state performed better than the other states, it also has the most variation across schools. Average school scores range from about 20 to 70 percent in mathematics and about 25 to 75 percent in language. The variation in average school scores in the other three states was much smaller.

As shown in table 5.3, differences between the average performance of girls and boys are not large. Only in two states was there a significant difference in scores: girls performed 4 percentage points higher than boys in Upper Nile and 3 percentage points lower in Western Bahr Ghazal.

Table 5.2 Student Performance in Mathematics and Language, 2009

State/score	Number	Mean %	Standard deviation
Average student test score in mathematics	**2,010**	**29**	**15.2**
Central Equatoria	719	27	11.2
Lakes	549	40	15.9
Upper Nile	430	21	15.1
Western Bahr Ghazal	312	28	11.8
Average student test score in language	**2,039**	**35**	**16.8**
Central Equatoria	793	33	13.3
Lakes	543	47	18.2
Upper Nile	412	24	12.9
Western Bahr Ghazal	291	32	14.2

Source: Analysis of SDS 2010.

Figure 5.2 School Average Test Score Distribution, Mathematics and Language, 2009

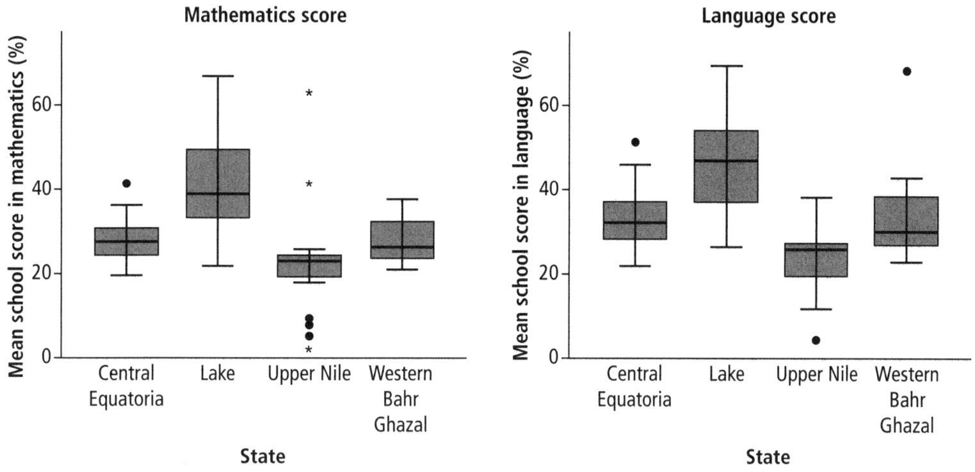

Source: Analysis of SDS 2010.
Note: The graph is read as follows: (a) the center line in the box plots indicates the median for the data set; (b) the lower and upper edges of the rectangle are the first and third quartiles of the data set; (c) the ends of the lines extending from the rectangle are the minimum and maximum values (excluding outliers); (d) the individual points represent potential outliers.

Table 5.3 Performance according to Gender, 2009

State		Mathematics (%)	Language (%)
Central Equatoria	Boy	27	33
	Girl	27	32
Lakes	Boy	41	49
	Girl	41	48
Upper Nile	Boy	23	26
	Girl	27	27
Western Bahr Ghazal	Boy	30	33
	Girl	27	32
Sample average	Boy	30	36
	Girl	29	34

Source: Analysis of SDS 2010.

Figure 5.3 portrays average student achievement according to four income groups or quartiles.[2] Quartile 1 is the poorest and quartile 4 the wealthiest. For all four quartiles, students in Lakes state performed, on average, higher than students in the same quartile in the other states.

Figure 5.3 Pupil Performance in Mathematics and Language according to Household Wealth

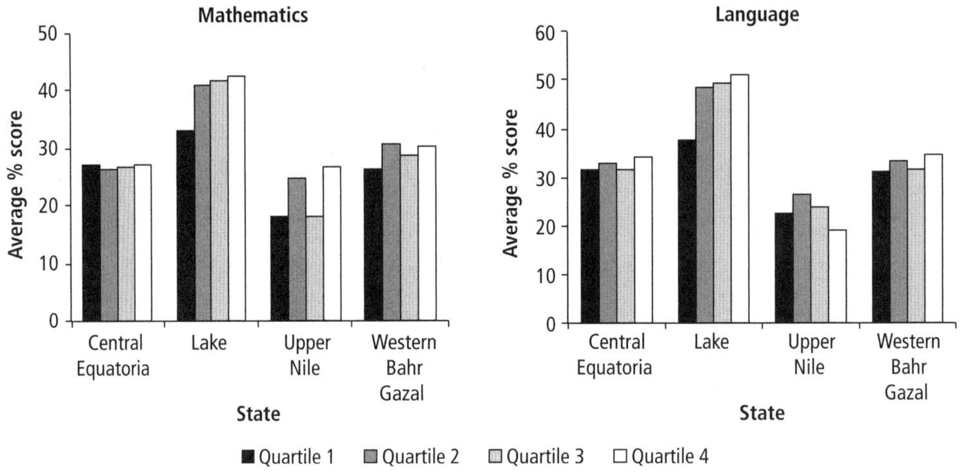

Source: Analysis of SDS 2010.

Except for language scores in Upper Nile, students in the wealthiest quartile generally performed better than those in the other quartiles. In some cases, in both mathematics and language, students from the second income quartile performed better than those in the third income quartile.

INTERNATIONAL COMPARISON OF STUDENT ASSESSMENT RESULTS

The Republic of South Sudan's performance in both mathematics and language is low compared to other countries. The 30 questions in the mathematics test administered in South Sudan included questions on knowing facts and procedures, on reasoning, on solving routine problems, and on using complex procedures and concepts. Table 5.4 lists the average score obtained for each group of questions for each of five countries and South Sudan. Solving routine problems and using complex procedures and concepts appear to be harder for students across countries. The tests were administered to grade 5 students in northern Sudan and Benin and grade 4 students in Yemen and Singapore. Considering that students mostly in the cities at the beginning of grade 6 took the test in South Sudan, performance is quite low when compared to other countries. If the rural schools in South Sudan are included in the sample, then the scores are likely to be much lower. Across the four categories, South Sudan's scores are lower than northern Sudan by an average of 8 percentage points. South Sudan does perform higher than Benin (except in reasoning) and Yemen.

Table 5.4   International Comparisons: Mathematics Average Score, 2009

Content area	Mean correct score for each content area (%)				
	The Republic of South Sudan	Northern Sudan	Benin	Yemen	Singapore
Grade in which test was administered	Grade 6	Grade 5	Grade 5	Grade 4	Grade 4
Knowing facts and procedures	31	39	23	28	81
Reasoning	38	47	41	36	85
Solving routine problems	28	31	22	24	79
Using complex procedures and concepts	27	37	20	26	70

Sources: Analysis of SDS 2010; IEA 2008.

The language test includes questions on documentary literature, on expository writing, and on narrative writing.[3] Few developing countries took this test; therefore, comparisons are only made with northern Sudan and Benin. The average performance for each group of questions for each country is given in table 5.5. Overall, narrative prose is more difficult than documentary or expository prose for most countries. South Sudan's scores are lower than northern Sudan by about 4 percentage points, on average. Benin, however, performs lower than South Sudan by about 6 percentage points.

SERVICE DELIVERY IN PRIMARY EDUCATION IN FOUR STATES

Student learning in primary education is dependent on the quality of service delivery in schools. This section, which for the most part is based on data for the four states examined in the Service Delivery Study,

Table 5.5   International Comparison of Student Performance in Language by Content Area, 2009

Content area	Mean correct score for each content area (%)			
	The Republic of South Sudan	Northern Sudan	Benin	Singapore
Grade in which test was administered	Grade 6	Grade 5	Grade 5	Grade 4
Document	37	39	32	83
Expository prose	43	44	32	82
Narrative prose	28	38	25	63

Sources: Analysis of SDS 2010; IEA 2008.

assessed the following basic components of service delivery in the education sector, without which instruction cannot adequately take place:

• physical infrastructure of schools (condition of school buildings, the availability of drinking water and toilets)
• classrooms and instructional materials (the availability of chalkboard, storage, desks, class sizes, textbooks, notebooks, and writing instruments)
• school management (school working days, record keeping, the curriculum used in schools, the pace of teachers' coverage of the curriculum, and teacher monitoring)
• community involvement evident in the participation and work of education councils in the education system.

SCHOOL INFRASTRUCTURE

This section looks at the status of primary school classrooms and the availability of drinking water and toilets in primary schools and finds that school facilities are generally inadequate. In particular, a third of classes are held under open air and half of schools lack access to drinking water and toilets.

Only one in four classrooms are permanent structures across South Sudan (table 5.6). This share varies between 14 and 15 percent in Jonglei and Warrap and 39 and 41 percent in Central Equatoria and Western Bahr Ghazal. Across South Sudan, a third of classes are held in open air, 2 percent in tents, and another 10 percent under roof only. The remaining

Table 5.6 Status of Primary School Classrooms, 2009

State	Type of structure (%)					
	Permanent	Semipermanent	Roof only	Tent	Open air	Other
Central Equatoria	39	29	11	1	18	1
Eastern Equatoria	32	18	15	2	31	1
Jonglei	15	36	5	1	42	1
Lakes	22	23	7	1	46	0
Northern Bahr Ghazal	20	28	11	2	37	1
Unity	22	28	6	1	42	0
Upper Nile	34	32	7	3	23	1
Warrap	14	46	6	1	32	0
Western Bahr Ghazal	41	26	14	2	17	1
Western Equatoria	26	13	20	2	38	1
The Republic of South Sudan	25	29	10	2	33	1

Source: Analysis of EMIS 2009.

about 30 percent of classes are held in semipermanent structures, typically made of mud, thatch, or grass. Schools without buildings, or in structures that cannot withstand rain, are unlikely to function for the whole school year, leading to the loss of instructional time. Moreover, particularly in open air schools, the level of distraction can be high due to people walking by or riding on bicycles or animals through or close to the school (UNICEF 2009).

A 2009 survey by the International Organization for Migration (IOM) provides data on the condition of schools in villages in three states. Over 90 percent of villages in Unity, Warrap, and Northern Bahr Ghazal were surveyed (table 5.7). Only 19 percent of villages surveyed in Unity, 18 percent in Warrap, and 27 percent in Northern Bahr Ghazal had a primary school. Some of the schools were not working, however; more than a third of schools in Unity were not working, while the shares of nonworking schools were just under 10 percent in Warrap and Northern Bahr Ghazal. Reasons given for the closure of schools included the destruction of school structure, no teachers, and no funds.

Table 5.7   Village Schools in Unity, Warrap, and Northern Bahr Ghazal, 2009

State	No. of villages surveyed	Villages with a school (%)	No. of working schools*	No. of nonworking schools *
Northern Bahr Ghazal	1,738 (96%)	27	488	45 (9%)
Unity	1,785 (100%)	19	374	134 (36%)
Warrap	2,049 (97%)	18	386	32 (8%)

Sources: IOM 2009a, 2009b, and 2009c.
Note: *Includes both primary and secondary schools in the villages surveyed.

According to EMIS data, about half of primary schools in South Sudan had access to drinking water and toilets in 2009 (table 5.8).[4] Across states, access to drinking water ranged from about 30 percent of schools in Upper Nile and Western Equatoria to more than 70 percent of schools in Lakes, Warrap, and Western Bahr Ghazal. The number of schools with toilets ranged from 33 percent in Unity to 70 percent in Western Bahr Ghazal. The UNICEF study (2009) also highlighted the limited availability of drinking water and toilets in schools.

CLASSROOMS AND INSTRUCTIONAL MATERIAL

This section looks at the availability of chalkboards, desks, and reading and writing materials in classrooms, and finds that many classrooms lack

Table 5.8 Drinking Water and Toilets in Primary Schools, 2009

State	Schools with drinking water (%)	Schools with toilet (%)
Central Equatoria	45	59
Eastern Equatoria	39	46
Jonglei	39	47
Lakes	69	46
Northern Bahr Ghazal	63	56
Unity	43	33
Upper Nile	32	41
Warrap	72	64
Western Bahr Ghazal	73	70
Western Equatoria	30	56
The Republic of South Sudan	49	51

Source: Analysis of EMIS 2009.

furniture, storage, and even basic instructional tools, such as a functional chalkboard. Average pupil-textbook ratios are generally 1:3.

Most classrooms surveyed in the Service Delivery Study did not have a functional chalkboard—a basic instructional tool. Across the four states, less than half the classrooms (40 percent) had chalkboards in good, usable condition (table 5.9).

Similarly, storage facilities are available in only 30 percent of classrooms surveyed in the Service Delivery Study: 20 percent in Central Equatoria, 19 percent in Lakes, 37 percent in Upper Nile, and 38 percent in Western Bahr Ghazal. When classrooms lack safe storage, it is a challenge for teachers to preserve their instructional aids or maintain records of student attendance and performance.

Table 5.9 Availability of Chalkboards and Storage in Classrooms in Four States, 2009

State	Classrooms with usable chalkboard (%)	Classrooms with safe storage (%)	Students with desks (%)
Central Equatoria	33	20	64
Lakes	37	19	20
Upper Nile	49	37	60
Western Bahr Ghazal	42	38	53
Sample average	40	29	53

Source: Analysis of SDS 2010.
Note: These data are based on grades 3, 4, and 5 observed in the sample schools.

The share of students that have a desk ranges from 20 percent in Lakes state to 64 percent in Central Equatoria. On average, across the four states, about half the students have desks.

In a situation where printed material for the most part is unavailable, textbooks constitute the only opportunity for children to practice reading and mathematics. In the Service Delivery Study, only a small percentage of students in the grade 3, 4, and 5 classrooms possessed a mathematics and language textbook (table 5.10). The availability of textbooks in Western Bahr Ghazal was particularly low (between 2 and 11 percent). In grades 4 and 5, a higher percentage of students in Lakes had textbooks (about 40 percent) when compared to the other three states. The pupil-to-textbook ratio for 2009 is available in the EMIS data for South Sudan

Table 5.10 Availability of Mathematics and Language Textbooks, 2009

Grade sampled	Pupils with a mathematics textbook (%)			Pupils with a language textbook (%)		
	Grade 3	Grade 4	Grade 5	Grade 3	Grade 4	Grade 5
Central Equatoria	16	17	12	18	16	12
Lakes	17	37	43	21	37	42
Upper Nile	23	19	23	18	21	25
Western Bahr Ghazal	4	4	3	6	11	2
Sample average	17	19	19	17	20	20

Source: Analysis of SDS 2010.

Table 5.11 Pupil-to-Textbook Ratio, 2009

State	Grades 1–4		Grades 5–8	
	Math	English	Math	English
Central Equatoria	1.6	1.6	4.8	3.9
Eastern Equatoria	2.9	3.0	3.5	3.7
Jonglei	3.1	2.8	8.0	2.4
Lakes	4.8	4.4	2.5	2.1
Northern Bahr Ghazal	4.7	4.1	4.4	3.4
Unity	8.0	6.9	9.4	4.0
Upper Nile	3.5	3.3	10.7	3.8
Warrap	6.5	6.2	3.8	3.9
Western Bahr Ghazal	2.2	2.3	9.6	1.7
Western Equatoria	2.2	2.1	3.7	2.2
The Republic of South Sudan	6.7	3.2	3.2	3.0

Source: Analysis of EMIS 2009.

(table 5.11). For grades 1–4 there were a few more English textbooks available than math textbooks. In English the ratio of textbook to pupil was 1:3 and in math it was 1:6.7. The ratio for math was better in 2008 (1:4.4.). For grades 5–8, the ratio for both math and English was 1:3, and this was an improvement from 2008 when it was 1:6.

Student opportunity for written practice reinforces learning. Like textbooks, notebooks (paper or exercise books) for writing practice are scarce. Between 10 and 17 percent of students in grade 3, 4, and 5 classrooms do not possess notebooks (table 5.12). The situation in Western Bahr Ghazal is ideal in grade 3 and grade 5 with 100 percent of students having notebooks. The availability of writing instruments is lower in other states, with pencils or pens available to about 72 percent of students in grades 3, 4, and 5 in Upper Nile; 81 percent in Lakes; 82 percent in Western Bahr Ghazal; and 83 percent in Central Equatoria.

Table 5.12   Availability of Mathematics and Language Notebooks and Writing Instruments, 2009

State	Students with a mathematics notebook (%)			Students with a language notebook (%)			Students with pencil/pen (%)
	Grade 3	Grade 4	Grade 5	Grade 3	Grade 4	Grade 5	
Central Equatoria	81	86	87	90	85	88	83
Lakes	88	93	87	85	79	85	81
Upper Nile	87	74	80	83	84	88	72
Western Bahr Ghazal	100	75	95	77	93	100	82
Average	86	83	86	86	85	89	79

Source: Analysis of EMIS 2009.

SCHOOL MANAGEMENT

This section looks at school working days, record keeping, curricula used, and syllabus coverage and presents these findings:

- There is large variability across schools and states in the number of days schools are in session.
- Most of the registered students were in school at the time of the survey.
- Teacher attendance on the day of the survey was less consistent than student attendance.
- Most teachers reported teaching less than 10 hours a day.
- Progress on syllabus coverage was generally low compared with planned progress.

There is considerable variation in the school year across states. According to the Service Delivery Study, 13 percent of schools reported closing

Table 5.13   Share of Schools Reporting Functioning Months, 2009

Start month	End month	Schools (%)
April	December	56
May	December	19
February	December	18
March	December	7

Source: Analysis of SDS 2010.

for three months during the school year and 7 percent for two months as a result of inclement weather. The number of months that schools functioned also varied across states and within states (table 5.13). Across the four states, 18 percent of schools functioned for 11 months (February to December), 7 percent for 10 months (March to December), 56 percent for 9 months (April to December), and 19 percent for 8 months (May to December). Different curricula could explain some of this variation in the number of months schools functioned. Notwithstanding, the length of the school year is quite short for those schools starting in April or May. Standardizing the number of working days per year across states and schools will be an important task for South Sudan.

When head teachers or principals were asked to report the number of working days during these months, they indicated a wide range: 110–288 days in Central Equatoria, 186–224 days in Lakes, 124–360 days in Upper Nile, and 151–299 days in Western Bahr Ghazal. Again, this indicates the lack of a standardized academic year across schools.

Except in Upper Nile, average student attendance was high in the classrooms observed for the Service Delivery Study. To compute student attendance, the number of students present on the day of the visit was compared to the number of students recorded in the attendance register. In Upper Nile, a third of the students were absent on the day of the visit. This could be due to the monsoons in progress during the study. In the Service Delivery Study an average of 12 percent of students in the classes observed were absent in Western Bahr Ghazal, 7 percent in Central Equatoria, and 3 percent in Lakes. In Lakes, there were more students in the grade 4 class than registered.

There is considerable variation in the extent to which schools maintain records on certain critical areas. The Service Delivery Study captures maintenance of school records in three key areas (table 5.14): student enrollment, student performance, and teacher leave. Records on student enrollment were maintained by 63 percent of schools in Upper Nile, 73

Table 5.14 Percentage of Schools Maintaining Records, 2009

| State | Schools able to show records (%) | | | Teachers' daily arrival and departure |
	Student enrollment	Student performance	Teachers' leave	
Central Equatoria	88	76	46	88
Lakes	96	85	81	93
Upper Nile	63	46	50	70
Western Bahr Ghazal	73	73	27	80
Sample average	82	70	53	83

Source: Analysis of SDS 2010.

percent in Western Bahr Ghazal, 88 percent in Central Equatoria, and 96 percent in Lakes. Fewer schools maintained records on student performance and even fewer on leave taken by teachers. A record of teachers' leave was kept by only 27 percent of schools in Western Bahr Ghazal, and half the schools in Upper Nile and Central Equatoria. This number was higher for Lakes (81 percent). Though more than 70 percent of schools kept a log of teacher arrival and departure, the discussion below shows the small percentage of teachers that arrive on time.

As mentioned earlier, a variety of curricula were adopted across states. Table 5.15 portrays the different curricula used in each state. MoE is in the process of introducing a national curriculum, and schools are gradually adopting it. In 2009, more than 60 percent of grade 4 classrooms had implemented the national curriculum, and more than 95 percent of grade 1 classrooms had done so.

Table 5.15 Type of Curricula Used in Grade 4, by State, 2009

State	The Republic of South Sudan	Ugandan	Ethiopian	Kenyan	Other
Central Equatoria	76	19	2	2	2
Eastern Equatoria	89	6	0	4	0
Jonglei	73	7	6	8	6
Lakes	62	8	8	13	8
Northern Bahr Ghazal	71	7	7	8	7
Unity	89	2	2	2	4
Upper Nile	91	3	2	2	2
Warrap	65	8	8	12	8
Western Bahr Ghazal	61	10	10	10	10
Western Equatoria	95	4	0	1	0
The Republic of South Sudan	76	8	5	7	5

Source: Analysis of EMIS 2009.

Figure 5.4   Teachers' Syllabus Coverage, 2009 Household Wealth

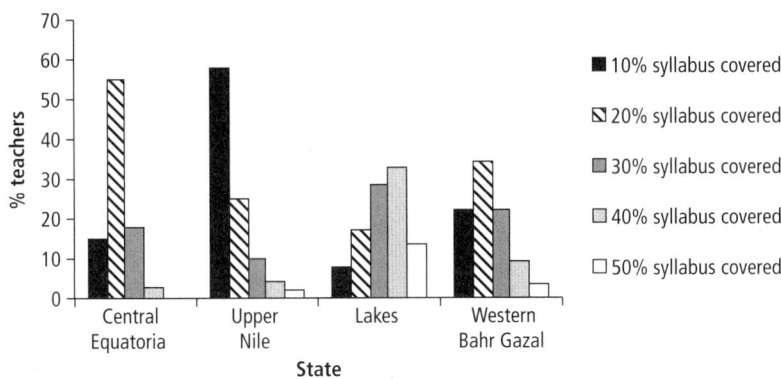

Source: Analysis of SDS 2010.

Teachers in South Sudan are expected to have an annual scheme that provides a road map for syllabus coverage over the school year and a lesson plan for the specific class period. An average of 71 percent of teachers across the four states had a plan for syllabus coverage, and over 88 percent claimed they instructed students based on a daily lesson plan. In spite of the existence of a scheme and lesson plans, syllabus coverage is not on schedule (figure 5.4). Even if schools started only in April or May, teachers at the time of the school visit for the Service Delivery Study should have completed about half the syllabus. In 2009, more than 70 percent of teachers in Central Equatoria and Upper Nile had completed less than 20 percent of the syllabus. The majority of teachers in Lakes and Western Bahr Ghazal were somewhat more on track.

Although most schools record teacher arrival and departure, many teachers do not arrive on time (table 5.16). The survey did not examine the extent to which teachers left the school early, but did examine (as reported by the principal) the number of teachers that arrived in school

Table 5.16   Teachers' Arrival and Departure, 2009

State	All teachers arriving on time last week (% of schools)	All teachers arriving on time last month (% of schools)	All teachers present at time of survey (% of schools)
Central Equatoria	15	15	32
Lakes	11	15	26
Upper Nile	17	38	42
Western Bahr Ghazal	29	14	21
Sample average	18	21	30

Source: Analysis of SDS 2010.

Table 5.17   Regular Teachers' Average Hours per Week, 2009

State	Percent of teachers teaching (hours per week)				
	3–10	11–20	21–30	31–40	Over 40
Central Equatoria	53	30	8	10	0
Lakes	19	21	33	21	6
Upper Nile	71	20	4	4	2
Western Bahr Ghazal	50	38	9	0	3

Source: Analysis of SDS 2010.

on time. In the week prior to the school visits, *all* teachers arrived on time in only 17 percent of schools in Upper Nile, 15 percent in Central Equatoria, 11 percent in Lakes, and 29 percent in Western Bahr Ghazal. In the previous month, the range of schools where all teachers arrived on time was from 21 percent in Western Bahr Ghazal to 42 percent in Upper Nile.

Instructional time is dependent not only on whether teachers are present, but also the distribution of instructional hours during the school day. During the school visits, all teachers were present in 42 percent of schools in Upper Nile, 32 percent in Central Equatoria, 26 percent in Lakes, and 21 percent in Western Bahr Ghazal. Table 5.17 provides the number of hours teachers instruct pupils in the classroom. According to teacher reports, the majority taught less than 10 hours per week: 71 percent of teachers in Upper Nile, 53 percent in Central Equatoria, and 50 percent in Western Bahr Ghazal. The story was different in Lakes, where the majority of teachers taught 21 to 30 hours per week.

Teachers in South Sudan take a large number of leave days each year (figure 5.5). It is not clear whether this leave is authorized officially or whether it is informal practice. It is likely the latter due to the absence of a leave policy in South Sudan, a situation discussed in more detail in chapter 7 on teacher management. In the Service Delivery Study, as only a few schools kept records on teachers' leave, headmasters' responses to the questions on teacher absence were incomplete and vague. According to answers given by teachers to the same questions, teachers take leave for a variety of reasons during the school year. About 24 percent of teachers across the four states took up to 4 days of sick leave in 2009, 16 percent took 5–10 days, and 4 percent took more than 10 days. For the illness of a family member, 32 percent of teachers took up to 4 days, 13 percent took 5–10 days, and 3 percent took more than 10 days. This proportion is similar for leave taken for social functions and emergencies. About 24 percent of teachers took up to 4 days for administrative and official tasks.

Figure 5.5   Teacher Leave—Reasons and Length of Absence, 2009

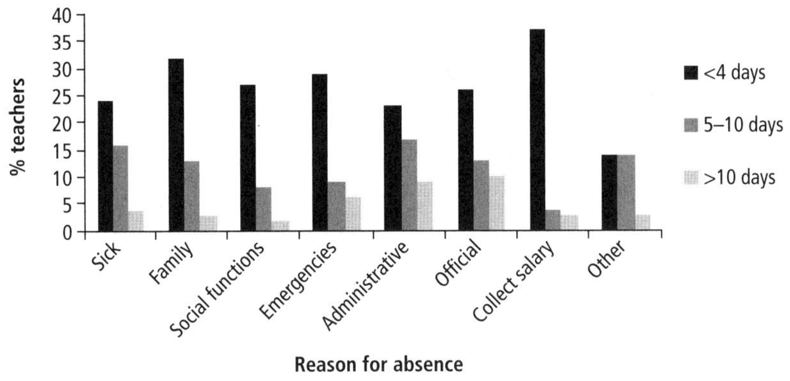

Source: Analysis of SDS 2010.

More teachers take between 5 and 10 days of leave for administrative tasks (17 percent) than for official tasks (13 percent). Taken together, teachers are absent for significant periods. Teacher absence is a more serious issue for schools where the school year is particularly short.

Teacher supervision by the head teacher and county inspector is less than satisfactory (table 5.18). Between 14 percent of teachers in Lakes and 31 percent in Upper Nile were never visited by the head teacher. Visits to teachers by the county inspector varied from 17 percent of teachers in Central Equatoria to 67 percent of teachers in the Upper Nile. A higher degree of monitoring in terms of the frequency of visits is evident in Lakes, followed by Central Equatoria. In both these states, the head teacher and the county inspector visit more than 80 percent of the teachers.

Table 5.18   Teacher Monitoring by the Head Teacher and County Inspector, 2009

State	Teachers visited by head teacher (%)			Teachers visited by county inspector (%)		
	Never	In the last 12 months	Last month	Never	In the last 12 months	Last month
Central Equatoria	17	8	75	17	42	42
Lakes	14	32	54	19	32	49
Upper Nile	31	5	64	67	19	14
Western Bahr Ghazal	15	5	80	55	20	25
Sample average	20	15	65	40	30	31

Source: Analysis of SDS 2010.

Table 5.19   Education Council Participation in Schools, 2009

State	Schools with an education council or PTA (%)	Education councils with an executive committee (%)	Committees that held one or more meetings last month (%)	Schools supported by local NGOs or institutions (%)
Central Equatoria	100	100	63	73
Lakes	88	85	81	58
Upper Nile	96	96	79	50
Western Bahr Ghazal	94	94	69	56
Sample average	95	94	72	61

Source: Analysis of SDS 2010.
Note: PTA = parent-teacher association; NGO = nongovernmental organization.

COMMUNITY INVOLVEMENT

Community participation in schools is strong. Across the four states, 95 percent of schools have an education council or parent-teacher association (PTA). In almost all cases, this organization is operating through an executive committee (table 5.19), and three-quarters of executive committees are reported to be active (holding meetings). About 60 percent of schools receive support from outside entities such as nongovernmental organizations (NGOs) and civil society.

The Service Delivery Study examined the kind of support that is provided by education councils and PTAs (table 5.20). Overall, support more often consists of helping teachers in the classroom, and less often of providing monetary support, such as paying for classroom supplies or even teacher salaries. This may in part be explained by widespread poverty, but could also be a result of the high frequency of school support provided by NGOs or other institutions as reported in table 5.19, which reduces the

Table 5.20   Types of Support Provided by Education Councils, 2009

State	% of schools in which executive committee			
	Helps teachers in the classroom	Buys textbooks	Buys learning material	Pays teacher salaries
Central Equatoria	33	5	10	33
Lakes	23	8	8	8
Upper Nile	33	0	25	4
Western Bahr Ghazal	31	0	13	6
Sample average	30	4	13	16

Source: Analysis of SDS 2010.

need for parents to contribute monetarily. The exception is the more urban Central Equatoria, in which a third of councils helped pay for teachers.

Table 5.20 suggests that parental contributions to education councils or PTAs are low in the schools surveyed, except those in Central Equatoria.

STUDENT LEARNING OUTCOMES IN SECONDARY EDUCATION

Table 5.21 presents data on student performance in secondary school examinations. Since secondary schools operate with different curricula, some students take an exam at the end of the third year, while others do so at the end of four years of secondary. No data are available for Warrap. In Eastern Equatoria, the number passed is higher than those registered, which suggests that some students took the exam without registering. Overall, around 60 percent of the 5,274 students who registered for the exam passed. This gives a total of about 3,300 students who passed the secondary school exam in 2009. Thus, the pipeline of students who could potentially continue in higher education is quite narrow.

Except in Western Equatoria and Western Bahr Ghazal, girls were generally less likely to pass the secondary school examination than boys. These two states also have the lowest pass rates overall.

Table 5.21 Examination Results in Secondary Education, 2009

State	Number registered	Passed (%)	
		Boys	Girls
Central Equatoria	1,138	82	76
Eastern Equatoria	349	105	79
Jonglei	493	83	76
Lakes	244	96	40
Northern Bahr Ghazal	2	100	
Unity	344	79	72
Upper Nile	1,675	63	45
Warrap			
Western Bahr Ghazal	497	14	40
Western Equatoria	532	21	21
The Republic of South Sudan	5,274	64	57

Source: Analysis of EMIS 2009.
Note: Data are from the exam at the end of secondary year 3 or secondary year 4, depending on the curriculum followed. Exam data from six-year secondary schools are excluded.

SERVICE DELIVERY IN SECONDARY EDUCATION

Information on service delivery in secondary education is scarce. The discussion below is based on available EMIS data on secondary schools. The physical structure; the availability of libraries, laboratories, and computers; and the curricula in use in different states were examined.

The majority of schools in secondary education function in concrete buildings (table 5.22). Warrap has the highest proportion of permanent structures. The proportion of permanent structures is slightly lower in Central Equatoria (69), Lakes (67), and Unity (58) than in the other states. An average of 18 percent of secondary schools operates in semipermanent structures across states. A few schools in Lakes, Upper Nile, Warrap, and Western Bahr Ghazal function in tents or in structures with just the roof in place.

About 66 percent of the secondary schools have access to drinking water and 82 percent to toilets. All schools in Unity and Western Equatoria have access to drinking water. Except in Northern Bahr Ghazal and Warrap, where only around 20 percent of schools have access to drinking water, in the other states about half the schools have access to drinking water. The availability of toilets ranges from 71 percent of schools in Eastern Equatoria to 100 percent of schools in Lakes. Whether there are sufficient toilets that are usable is not known.

Table 5.22 Secondary School Infrastructure, 2009

State	% of school structures that are:				
	Permanent	Semipermanent	Roof only	Tent	Open air
Central Equatoria	69	26	2	0	2
Eastern Equatoria	89	7	0	0	4
Jonglei	76	24	0	0	0
Lakes	67	28	4	0	0
Northern Bahr Ghazal	77	23	0	0	0
Unity	58	29	0	0	14
Upper Nile	78	17	4	1	0
Warrap	92	0	0	8	0
Western Bahr Ghazal	84	10	0	1	5
Western Equatoria	89	8	0	0	3
The Republic of South Sudan	78	18	1	1	2

Source: Analysis of EMIS 2009.

Table 5.23   Libraries, Laboratories, and Computers in Secondary Schools, 2009

State	Schools having libraries (%)	% of schools having laboratories in:				Schools with computers (%)
		Physics	Biology	Chemistry	Combined science	
Central Equatoria	27	7	4	7	11	7
Eastern Equatoria	12	12	12	12	12	6
Jonglei	0	0	0	0	0	0
Lakes	60	20	20	20	20	0
Northern Bahr Ghazal	12	0	0	0	0	0
Unity	25	0	0	0	0	0
Upper Nile	0	0	0	0	0	0
Warrap	0	0	0	0	0	0
Western Bahr Ghazal	7	7	7	7	0	0
Western Equatoria	11	6	6	0	11	6
The Republic of South Sudan	8	5	4	4	6	3

Source: Analysis of EMIS 2009.

There is a critical shortage of libraries and laboratories (table 5.23). Lakes has a higher number of libraries and laboratories when compared to the other states. No school has a library in Jonglei, Upper Nile, and Warrap. Excluding these states, approximately 8 percent of schools have a library. Only four states—Central and Eastern Equatoria, and Northern and Western Bahr Ghazal—have science laboratories, and even in these states only an average of about six schools has a laboratory. A handful of schools across the three states have computers.

A variety of curricula are in use in secondary education in South Sudan. Apart from the South Sudan curriculum, which has been adopted by 58 percent of schools, others use the Kenyan and Ugandan curricula (table 5.24). Seven percent of schools use the Kenyan curriculum, 21 percent use the Ugandan, and 14 percent of schools use other curricula. The South Sudan curriculum appears to be the most popular and is used by 58 percent of schools. The majority of schools in Upper Nile (90 percent) and Western Bahr Ghazal (100 percent) use the South Sudan curriculum. In Unity, 88 percent of schools use a different curriculum. The Ugandan curriculum is most popular in Central Equatoria and the Kenyan curriculum in Lakes.

Table 5.24   Curricula in Secondary Schools, 2009

State	% of schools with the following curriculum:			
	Kenyan	The Republic of South Sudan	Ugandan	Other
Central Equatoria	4	39	46	11
Eastern Equatoria	4	64	31	1
Jonglei	15	42	0	42
Lakes	39	43	18	0
Northern Bahr Ghazal	28	61	0	11
Unity	0	14	0	86
Upper Nile	0	90	0	10
Warrap	15	30	20	35
Western Bahr Ghazal	0	100	0	0
Western Equatoria	3	70	10	16
The Republic of South Sudan	7	58	21	14

Source: Analysis of EMIS 2009.

KEY FINDINGS

- Although student pass rates at the primary school examination are high—perhaps because examinations often test the more able students—**a test of student learning in grade 6 in a sample of mostly urban schools in four states finds weak levels of student learning in both language and mathematics**. In language, students got 35 percent of questions right, while in mathematics, students answered correctly 29 percent of the time.[5]
- **These results are no surprise, given the history of education in the Republic of South Sudan** and considering that many other countries in Sub-Saharan Africa and other parts of the world are struggling with achieving good levels of student learning. Comparing the South Sudan's sample with results found in other developing countries that have used the same or similar tests, we find that South Sudan's school sample performed a little better than Benin, on par with the Republic of Yemen, but not as good as northern Sudan.[6]
- **The report documents weaknesses in service delivery in primary and secondary schools, which likely contribute to the weak learning performance**. Most of the primary schools and some of the secondary schools do not have permanent structures leading to the loss of school working days. There is a shortage of drinking water and toi-

lets, especially in primary schools. Average class sizes are high in primary schools, which makes instruction a challenge. There is a severe shortage of textbooks in both primary and secondary schools. According to the Service Delivery Study, two-thirds of the students did not have paper to write on and a fifth of the students did not have writing instruments—limiting opportunities for reinforcing what is taught.

- **The report has documented weak school management practices in several areas**:
  - There is no clear policy on the number of working days in a school year and some of the schools functioned for less than eight months.
  - Record-keeping associated with enrollments, student performance, and teachers' leave is not uniform.
  - Inadequate instruction is evident in the slow coverage of the syllabus in classrooms, which leads to a cumulative shrinkage of what students learn each year.
  - Tardiness of teachers and a very limited number of hours teachers spend on instruction per week can explain the slow pace of syllabus coverage.
  - Only about half the head teachers and county inspectors monitor teachers in classrooms. Improving the functioning of schools in these areas is critical to improve educational outcomes, retention, and learning.

NOTES

1. In Benin and northern Sudan, these tests were given to students in grade 5. They were tested in the same selection of test questions as the Republic of South Sudan.

2. For the construction of the asset index, each of nine assets was assigned a weight equal to the fraction of pupils that own the asset. The assets included *a car, a refrigerator, a electricity, tap water, a television, a radio, a computer, a mobile phone, and a gas or electric stove.* If the number of possessions = 0, then index = 1 (poorest); if the number of possessions >=5, then index = 4 (wealthiest).

3. A *document* is a circumscribed representation of a body of information that one can or intends to communicate. *Expository writing* uses a style that can inform, explain, describe, or define the author's subject to the reader. This kind of writing is often used in academics to demonstrate knowledge and familiarity with the topic or subject. *Narrative writing* tells a story or part of a story. Narrative writing is used in novels, short stories, biographies, autobiographies, historical accounts, essays, poems, and plays.

4. The survey did not examine the quality of the drinking water or whether the toilets were usable.

5. Both tests were multiple choice tests, in which randomly filled test questionnaires would give an average score of around 25 percent.

6. However, the Republic of South Sudan as a whole would likely produce weaker results, since most of the country's schools are rural, while the sample included mainly urban schools.

CHAPTER 6

Education Spending

Thisthis chapter analyzes the patterns of education spending in the Republic of South Sudan. The focus is on public spending, but some figures for private spending are also provided. Information on donor spending is not included for lack of information. First, the trend in public education spending since 2006 is shown. Next, the chapter focuses in more detail on the patterns of public education spending in 2009, calculates per student spending by level of education, analyzes its composition, and compares it with per student spending in other countries in the region. Finally, estimates of the volume of household spending on education are provided.

TREND IN PUBLIC EDUCATION SPENDING SINCE 2006

This section analyzes the trend in public spending since 2006, the first full year of the Government of the Republic of South Sudan (GoRSS), because this is the time when public education spending really started in South Sudan. During the conflict years, the school network was smaller and composed primarily of community or religious schools, or schools supported by nongovernmental organizations (NGOs), many functioning with the help of volunteer teachers. Since around 2005, GoRSS has been building a network of government or government-supported schools that have civil servant teachers, although many volunteers still remain in the system. GoRSS is now financing the salaries of some 30,000 education staff working in schools and administrative offices across the states. GoRSS is counting on donors to cover most of the capital spending and support schools with instructional materials, school feeding, and so forth.

The annual budget of GoRSS (blue book) captures both (a) the education spending at the central level, represented by the Ministry of Education (MoE) budget, and (b) the transfers from central GoRSS to the 10 states to support the provision of education (known as conditional transfers, education part). Funded mainly by this transfer, states are responsible for running most government schools at the primary and secondary levels and Alternative Education System (AES) learning centers.[1] In principle, the states have some taxing authority and are supposed to top off the funds received from the conditional transfer, but states have made it known they do not have their own revenues to invest in education and are thus only funding schools with the transfer.[2] Thus, government spending is for the most part captured in the GoRSS' annual budget books.

As a result of a budgetary crisis, GoRSS education spending has been declining since 2008, but the budget priority for education has been more or less stable since 2006. Table 6.1 presents data on aggregate GoRSS education spending since 2006. It also shows the share of the total GoRSS spending that is allocated to education. Corrected for inflation, GoRSS' education spending has dropped from the SDG 270 million–290 million range between 2006 and 2008 to only SDG 207 million in 2009 and a budgeted SDG 254 million for 2010 (all in constant 2008 SDG). The drop in 2009 is explained by a strong decline in oil prices in the wake of the global financial crisis. In terms of the budget share allocated to education, the share fluctuates in the 5–8 percent range without any particular trend, although it seems education was harder hit than other sectors by the 2009 budget crisis (8 percent of the 2009 budget was originally allocated to education but only 6 percent was actually spent). For 2010, education's share of the total GoRSS budget is again 8 percent, indicating that education is still a GoRSS spending priority.

The decline in education spending is happening at a time when the school-age population is growing; this has led to a considerable drop in public spending per child. Figure 6.1 shows the trend in GoRSS education

Table 6.1 Trend in GoRSS Education Spending, 2006–10

Spending	2006 Actual	2007 Actual	2008 Actual	2009 Approved budget	2009 Actual (provisional)	2010 Approved budget
In current SDG million	225.2	233.1	290.2	291.3	234.1	323.5
In constant 2008 SDG million	279.0	269.8	290.2	258.0	207.3	254.2
As % of total GoRSS spending	6	8	5	8	6	8

Sources: MoFEP's budget books, 2007–10.

Figure 6.1   Trend in Public Education Spending per Child (Ages 6–16), 2006–09

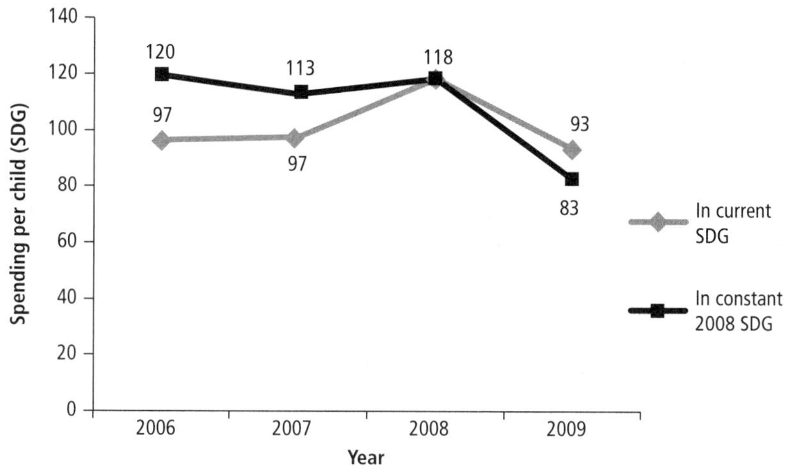

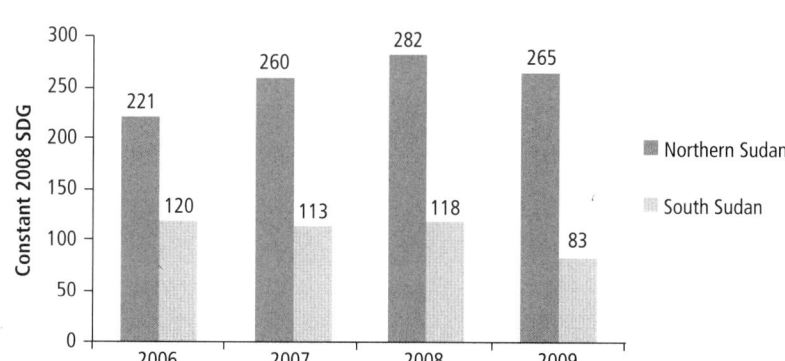

Sources: MoFEP's budget books, 2007–10. Data for 2006–08 are actuals, for 2009 provisional.

spending per school-aged child (age 6–16), calculated by dividing total GoRSS education spending by the population of that age group. In real terms, spending per child declined from SDG 120 in 2006 to SDG 83 in 2009, a 30 percent drop.

Figure 6.2 compares the trend in spending per child with the corresponding figures for northern Sudan. In 2006, education spending per child was almost twice as much in northern Sudan than in South Sudan; by 2009, northern Sudan was spending three times as much per school-age child. This difference reflects a far more developed education system

Figure 6.2   Comparison of Public Education Spending per Child (Ages 6–16), in Northern Sudan and the Republic of South Sudan, 2006–09

Sources: Figure 6.1 and World Bank 2012.

in the north with a significant and growing share of youth continuing their studies up through to higher education. It also seems to reflect that northern Sudan was not as affected as South Sudan by the drop in oil prices because of their more diversified economy.

ANALYSIS OF PUBLIC EDUCATION SPENDING IN 2009

This section focuses on the patterns of spending in a single year, 2009. The purpose of the analysis is to assess how spending is allocated across levels of education and by type of spending to provide a better understanding of how resources are used. The analysis is based as much as possible on actual spending rather than budget figures, since these often differ widely.

RECURRENT AND CAPITAL SPENDING BY LEVEL OF GOVERNMENT

In 2009, GoRSS spent 97 percent of the education budget on recurrent costs and 77 percent on staff salaries. Table 6.2 provides a first, simple breakdown of GoRSS education spending—this breakdown is readily available in GoRSS' budget books. In 2009, 97 percent of total public education spending was recurrent and 3 percent was capital spending. The share for capital spending was unusually low that year due to the budget crisis, as capital spending was cut more than recurrent spending in an effort to protect staff salaries (capital spending was cut from a budgeted SDG 40 million to SDG 6 million in 2009). The recurrent spending has two parts, salaries and operating expenses; salaries represent 77 percent and operations 21 percent of total education spending. Thus, almost four out of every five pounds invested by GoRSS in education goes to salaries. The remaining pound goes largely to recurrent operating expenses other than salaries.

Table 6.2 GoRSS Education Spending by Spending Category and Level of Government, 2009

In SDG million (2009 provisional)	Recurrent		Capital	Total spending	
	Salaries	Operating		SGD million	%
MoE	10.3	47.6	6.2	64.1	27
Transfer to states for education	169.4	0.7	0.0	170.0	73
Total spending SDG million	179.7	48.3	6.2	234.1	100
%	77	21	3	100	—

Source: MoFEP's budget book 2010.
Note: — Not available.

The education sector is very decentralized in terms of the volume of spending that is administered by the states. Table 6.2 also shows that almost three-quarters (73 percent) of the education budget was spent by the states, mainly to cover salaries. The budget share transferred to the states for their spending needs is higher than in most other sectors in South Sudan. On paper, the states spend their resources almost exclusively on salaries (SDG 169.4 million out of a total transfer of SDG 170 million) since they are allocated only a tiny operating budget (SDG 0.7 million) and no capital budget. But in the absence of other sources of revenue, funds are likely somewhat fungible and states may be forced to dip into the transfer for salaries to fund minor recurrent operating costs. States have been lobbying for larger operating budgets, but in the current budget environment GoRSS has not been able to finance this.

MoE's central budget is well documented, but represents only a quarter of public education spending because most public education spending goes through the states. The MoE has a salary budget that covers staff working in the ministry, in three teacher training institutes,[3] in three other national institutes of education,[4] in the 10 National Secondary Schools, and in the mobile AES centers (giving a total salary budget of SDG 10.3 million in 2009). MoE also has a fairly large operating budget (SDG 47.6 million). The government's budget books include fairly detailed descriptions of the programs funded by MoE's operating budget, but MoE's budget is small compared with the states' spending. Other than the information used for table 6.2, there is no other public information on how the totality of education resources is spent. For example, there is no readily available information on the breakdown of spending by level of education: primary, secondary, AES, and so forth. Therefore, information from different sources had to be pieced together for the breakdown of spending by level of education provided in the next section.

DISTRIBUTION OF RECURRENT SPENDING BY LEVEL OF EDUCATION

Table 6.3 estimates the breakdown of public recurrent spending by level of education. It is based on several different data sources: most important, on a detailed review of the 2009 payroll database of each state to determine how many staff work in pre-primary, primary, or secondary schools, or in AES learning centers.[5] To have a more complete picture of education spending, higher education spending data were collected from the Government of National Unity (GoNU) in Khartoum and through a visit to Juba University.

Table 6.3   Approximate Breakdown of Public Recurrent Education Spending by Level of Education, 2009

Education level	Total, SDG million	Share, incl. GoNU (%)	Share, GoRSS only (%)
Pre-primary	1.8	0.7	0.8
Primary	154.2	54.8	67.6
Secondary	49.6	17.6	21.7
AES	19.2	6.8	8.4
Teacher training institutes (TTI)	3.1	1.1	1.4
Higher education support from GoRSS	0.3	0.1	0.1
Total supported by GoRSS	**228.2**	**81.1**	**100**
Higher education funding from GoNU	*53.3*	*18.9*	—
Total, including funding from GoNU	***281.5***	***100***	—

Source: Estimation based on analysis of 2009 budget execution data, the payroll database, and information on higher education provided by Juba University and GoNU.
Note: Figures include MoE's central budget broken down and distributed across levels of education by prorating with each education level's salary spending.
— Not available.

In 2009, primary education received 55 percent; secondary, 18 percent; and higher education, 19 percent of total public recurrent education spending. The three public universities in South Sudan are mainly funded by GoNU (grants amounting to SDG 53 million in 2009 according to GoNU data) but also receive minor support from GoRSS MoE (an estimated SDG 0.3 million in 2009). When higher education spending is included, total public education spending in 2009 increases from the SDG 228 million included in GoRSS' recurrent education budget to a total of SDG 281 million. Out of this total, less than 1 percent goes to pre-primary education, 55 percent to primary education, 18 percent to secondary education, 7 percent to AES, 1 percent to teacher training institutes (TTIs), and 19 percent to higher education. For completeness, the last column in table 6.3 shows the percentage breakdown of GoRSS education spending by level of education.

The first six years of the primary cycle receive at least 45 percent of total recurrent education spending. South Sudan allocates 55 percent of recurrent education spending to the eight-year primary cycle; this gives an average spending per year of primary school of 6.9 percent of total recurrent education spending. If all schools offered all the primary grades, we would calculate the cost of the first six years of primary education to 41 percent of total recurrent spending (calculated as 6.9 × 6). Given the many schools that do not have grades 7 and 8, however, it is fair to assume that at least 45 percent of the budget goes to the first six years, maybe even as much as 50 percent.

The share of spending allocated to the first six years of primary education in South Sudan is quite similar to that of many other countries in the region, as shown in table 6.4. The low-income countries shown, Chad, Ethiopia, and Kenya, allocate a similar share of their budgets to the first six years of primary education (48 percent, 51 percent, and 55 percent respectively) as South Sudan (45–50 percent). The lower-middle-income countries, including Cape Verde, Côte d'Ivoire, and Lesotho, allocate slightly lower shares (39 percent, 43 percent, and 36 percent respectively), as these countries tend to have larger secondary and higher education enrollments. With respect to the shares allocated to upper secondary and higher education, the variation across countries is much wider and without a clear pattern for low- and middle-income countries. The distribution of spending across these levels depends more on the policy choices of individual countries.

The public universities mainly rely on public funding but also generate their own revenues from student fees. Table 6.5 provides the total rev-

Table 6.4   Regional Comparison of Public Spending by Level of Education, LAY

	Share of public recurrent education spending (%)		
State/region	Primary (adjusted to 6 years)	Secondary (upper[b])	Higher
The Republic of South Sudan	45–50[a]	18	19
Northern Sudan	372	16	30
SSA low-income countries			
Chad	48	12	23
Ethiopia	51	8	20
Kenya	55	12	16
SSA lower-middle-income countries			
Cape Verde	39	16	12
Côte d'Ivoire	43	10	21
Lesotho	36	11	37
MENA lower-middle-income countries			
Egypt, Arab Rep.	40	n.a.	39
Morocco	46	19	16
Tunisia	35	22	22

Sources: World Bank EdStats; Pôle de Dakar 2010; Majgaard and Mingat 2012; World Bank 2012.
Note: Data are for latest available year, none before 2005. LAY = latest available year; MENA = Middle East and North Africa; n.a. = Not available; SSA = Sub-Saharan Africa.
a. The share of primary education in total public education spending is adjusted to six years for South Sudan and northern Sudan and data are for six years of primary education for all other countries shown.
b. The comparison is done for the upper-secondary level, since South Sudan does not have lower-secondary education due to the longer primary cycle (eight years).

Table 6.5 Revenues and Expenditures of the Republic of South Sudan's Public Universities, 2009–10

Revenues (SDG million)	Grants from GoNU	Own revenues	Other	Total
University of Juba	24.4	13.1		37.5
Upper Nile University	13.2	0.8	0.1	14.1
Bahr El Ghazal University	11.0	0.6		11.5
Social subsidy[a]	4.7			4.7
Total, including	**53.3**	**14.5**	**0.1**	**67.9**
own revenues	**78.5%**	**21.3%**	**0.1%**	**100%**
Expenditures (SDG million)	Salary	Nonsalary operating	Social subsidy[a]	Total
University of Juba	27.2	9.8		37.0
Upper Nile University	12.6	1.5		14.1
Bahr El Ghazal University	9.7	2.4		12.1
Social subsidy[a]			4.7	4.7
Total, including own revenues	49.4	13.8	4.7	67.9
Public expenditures	**38.0**	**10.6**	**4.7**	**53.3**
(estimated)	**71.2%**	**19.9%**	**8.9%**	**100%**

Source: Analysis of data from GoNU's Federal Ministry for Higher Education and Scientific Research.
Note: a. World Bank estimate based on figures for GoNU's total social subsidies provided to higher education students. The three universities' share is calculated by prorating based on enrollments at their campuses in the north.

enues of each of the three public universities, including own resources. The total budget for all three amounts to SDG 67.9 million in 2009–10. Of this, SDG 14.5 million are funded through own revenue generation, while GoNU supported the three universities with SDG 53.3 million. Thus, government grants represent 79 percent of the universities' funding and own revenues, mainly generated from student fees, represent 21 percent. The second part of table 6.5 presents the breakdown of expenditures of the public universities, by salaries, nonsalary operating spending, and social subsidies. As shown, a little more than 70 percent go to salaries, 20 percent to nonsalary operating expenses, and 9 percent to social subsidies to support students' living expenses.

COMPOSITION OF RECURRENT SPENDING BY LEVEL OF EDUCATION

Table 6.6 is based on table 6.3, but also shows the composition of recurrent spending at each level of education.[6] For this table, simple assumptions were made about the distribution of the operating budget across levels of education (by prorating with salaries), and so the operating

Table 6.6   Composition of Public Recurrent Spending at Each Level of Education, 2009

Level of education	In SDG million			
	Salary	Operating	Social subsidy	Total
Pre-primary	1.5	0.4	—	1.8
Primary	121.5	32.7	—	154.2
Secondary	39.1	10.5	—	49.6
AES	15.1	4.1	—	19.2
Teacher training Institutes (TTI)	2.5	0.7	—	3.1
Higher education support from GoRSS	—	—	0.3	0.3
Total supported by GoRSS	**179.7**	**48.3**	**0.3**	**228.2**
Higher education funding from GoNU	38.0	10.6	4.7	53.3
Total	**217.7**	**59.0**	**5.0**	**281.5**

Source: Estimation based on analysis of MoE's 2009 budget data, the states' payroll database, and data on higher education spending collected from the GoNU's Federal Ministry for Higher Education and Scientific Research.

spending figures are very approximate. In terms of the distribution of salaries by level of education, the two largest spending blocks are salaries in primary and secondary education, at SDG 121.5 million and SDG 39.1 million, respectively; then follows salaries in higher education at SDG 38.0 million and AES at SDG 15.1 million.

ANALYSIS OF THE PAYROLL IN THE 10 STATES

This section analyzes in more detail the spending on salaries in the 10 states. This is of particular interest because most of public education spending goes to salaries (77 percent). For the sake of completeness, the analysis also provides figures on the number of education staff not on payroll in the states, the volunteers.

The analysis draws on two sources of data, the payroll database for the states and the EMIS database. Both are needed to establish a full picture of education sector staff working in the states, as the payroll does not include the volunteers, and because EMIS includes only staff working in schools (in the following discussion we call these school-based staff: they include both teachers and nonteaching staff working in schools). Many education sector staff also work in the education offices of the states, counties, or *payams*, and thus are identified as "nonschool based."

The education payroll of all the states included a total of 30,616 personnel in 2009; 80 percent of them work in schools. Figure 6.3 presents a breakdown of staff who are included in the payroll in the states. In 2009,

Figure 6.3 Number of Staff on Payroll in All States, by Workplace, 2009

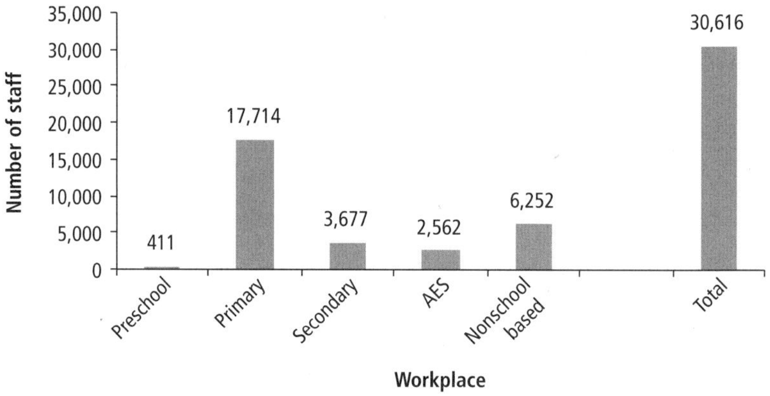

Source: Analysis of the payroll database.

there was a total of 30,616 education staff on government payroll across the 10 states. Of the total, 1 percent (411) were working in preschools, 58 percent (17,714) in primary schools, 12 percent (or 3,677) in secondary schools, and 8 percent (2,562) in AES; 20 percent (6,252) were non-school-based staff. The nonschool-based staff are typically education officers, inspectors, or support staff.

Distribution of paid staff across states is inconsistent with the states' share of total enrollments. If a state has 10 percent of the total student enrollments of South Sudan, it would be consistent that the state would also have around 10 percent of the total number of paid staff working in states (more or less; some adjustments may be needed for states with large secondary enrollments and so forth). Figure 6.4 depicts the 10 states by their share of enrollments and their share of staff. Five states each have more or less 10 percent of South Sudan's student enrollments (Northern Bahr Ghazal, Warrap, Unity, Eastern Equatoria, and Central Equatoria, all in the horizontal circle). But their share of total paid staff varies between 8 percent in Northern Bahr Ghazal and 21 percent in Central Equatoria. This indicates that there is scope for improving staff and payroll management at the central GoRSS level, where the distributions across states are decided.

Jonglei, Northern Bahr Ghazal, and Upper Nile have relatively few paid staff, while the three Equatoria states have relatively many. Table 6.7 presents the same data, but includes a column that checks the consistency between the share of staff and share of students. As shown, the three Equatoria states all have more staff than their enrollment shares would justify, while Jonglei, Northern Bahr Ghazal, and Upper Nile have much less staff than they should based on their student enrollments. This is a

Figure 6.4   Distribution of Paid Staff and Enrollments across the 10 States, 2009

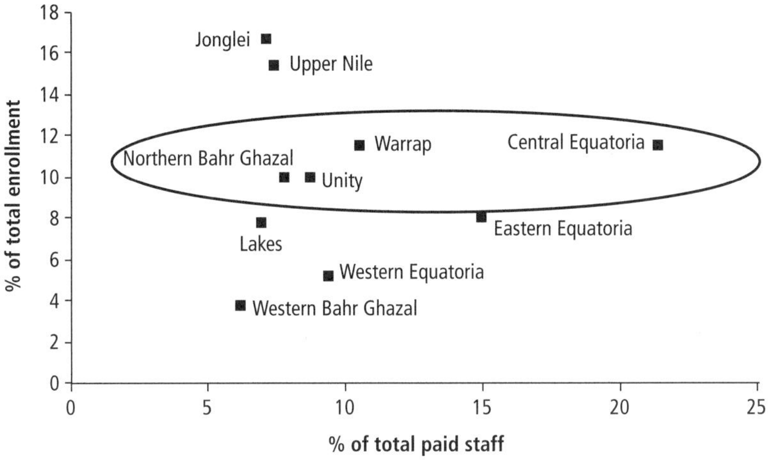

Source: Analysis of the payroll database and EMIS 2009 data.

Table 6.7   Consistency between Distribution of Paid Staff and Enrollments across the States, 2009

State	Share of total enrollments at all levels (%)	Share of total education staff on state payroll (%)	Result of consistency check
Central Equatoria	12	21	High share of staff
Eastern Equatoria	8	15	High share of staff
Jonglei	17	7	Low share of staff
Lakes	8	7	Proportionate
Northern Bahr Ghazal	10	8	Low share of staff
Unity	10	9	Proportionate
Upper Nile	15	7	Low share of staff
Warrap	11	10	Proportionate
Western Bahr Ghazal	4	6	High share of staff
Western Equatoria	5	9	High share of staff
Total	100	100	

Source: Data on staff are from the payroll database. Data on enrollment share are from the NBHS 2009.

rough check only, and other criteria than just enrollments should be taken into account when distributing staff, including, for example, school-age population and the distribution of enrollments by level of schooling.

Across the 10 states, the share of staff that do not work in schools varies between 12 and 44 percent of the education payroll. Table 6.8 shows the number of staff working in each of the 10 states by workplace.

Table 6.8 Number of Staff on Payroll in Each State, by Workplace, 2009

| State | Number of school-based staff | Nonschool-based staff | | Total |
		Number	% of total	
Central Equatoria	5,419	1,089	17	6,508
Eastern Equatoria	3,974	577	13	4,551
Jonglei	1,748	424	20	2,172
Lakes	1,771	354	17	2,125
Northern Bahr Ghazal	1,880	503	21	2,383
Unity	2,354	309	12	2,663
Upper Nile	1,563	690	31	2,253
Warrap	2,611	597	19	3,208
Western Bahr Ghazal	1,059	836	44	1,895
Western Equatoria	2,233	625	22	2,858
Total	24,612	6,004	20	30,616

Source: Data on staff are from the payroll database. Data on enrollment share are from the NBHS 2009.

The share of staff that are nonschool based varies widely around the South Sudanese average of 20 percent. In Upper Nile (one of the states that might have too few staff), almost a third of staff are not working in any school, and in Western Bahr Ghazal (which might have too many staff), the share of nonschool-based staff is as much as 44 percent. On the other hand, Unity and Eastern Equatoria have only 12–13 percent of their paid staff working in offices rather than schools. This suggests that each state manages its payroll very differently and that there could be scope for improvement in some states more than in others.

Overall, 28 percent of staff on payroll in the states are Category A, 44 percent are Category B, and 29 percent are support staff (Category C). Table 6.9 distinguishes between three categories of staff based on salary grade. The first category, Category A, includes the better paid civil servant staff (grade 10 and lower). Category B includes junior civil servants, such as primary teachers just starting out (grade 14) or just appointed after 18 months of provision employment (grade 12). Category C includes staff in grades 11, 13, 15, or higher, which corresponds to support or unclassified staff, such as workers, cleaners, drivers, and so forth.

In primary education, there is a relatively higher proportion of Category B staff (which make up 56 percent), while secondary education has

Table 6.9 Distribution of Paid Education Staff in the States, by Staff Category, 2009

Category	Number of staff
School-based staff	24,612
Primary education	19,864
Category A (classified, higher pay)	19%
Category B (classified, lower pay)	56%
Category C (unclassified)	25%
Secondary education	4,748
Category A	41%
Category B	25%
Category C	33%
Nonschool-based staff	6,004
Category A	44%
Category B	18%
Category C	38%
Total staff on payroll in states	30,616
Category A	28%
Category B	44%
Category C	29%

Source: Analysis of the payroll database.
Note: Category A: Salary grade <=10: classified staff with higher salary (such as managers, secondary teachers).
Category B: Salary grade = 12 or 14: classified staff with lower salary (such as primary teachers).
Category C: Salary grade = 11, 13, or >=15: unclassified staff (such as cleaners, drivers, support staff).

relatively more Category A (41 percent) and support staff (33 percent). This reflects that secondary teachers typically require a higher level of education and are in a higher pay grade than primary teachers. Also, secondary schools typically have more support staff than primary schools, as they more often have cafeterias, laboratories, gardens, or other facilities that need management and maintenance. Among the nonschool-based staff, most are either higher paid civil servants (44 percent) or support staff (38 percent).

Primary school staff were paid about SDG 5,000 and secondary school staff about SDG 7,000, on average, in 2009, according to table 6.10. These figures include all staff types except those not on payroll (volunteers). But average annual salaries in primary and secondary schools differ widely across states. For primary education, the highest average salary is in Northern Bahr Ghazal (SDG 8,301), which is more than twice as much as Eastern Equatoria (SDG 3,592) and Central Equatoria (SDG 3,834). Part

Table 6.10 Estimated Average Salaries in Primary and Secondary Education by State, 2009

State	Average annual salary (SDG)		Average salary (SDG) (indexed to average salary for the Republic of South Sudan as a whole)	
	Primary	Secondary	Primary	Secondary
Central Equatoria	3,834	5,070	78	72
Eastern Equatoria	3,592	7,535	73	108
Jonglei	5,857	7,676	119	110
Lakes	4,957	5,327	101	76
Northern Bahr Ghazal	8,301	5,700	168	81
Unity	6,507	12,081	132	172
Upper Nile	6,664	7,009	135	100
Warrap	4,623	9,102	94	130
Western Bahr Ghazal	6,886	8,172	140	117
Western Equatoria	4,327	8,434	88	120
Total	4,932	7,005	100	100

Source: Estimation based on analysis of the payroll database.
Note: Data are for school-based staff, teachers as well as nonteachers, volunteers excluded.

of these differences may be explained by differences in the composition of staff across the states, with some states having more or less of the different staff categories. But it may also be that the salary grid for civil servants in South Sudan, which in principle is uniform for all states, is not fully implemented everywhere.

Table 6.10 also shows the average salaries in primary and secondary education in multiples of GDP per capita. For South Sudan, however, the choice of GDP per capita for this calculation is not obvious, as discussed in chapter 1. Therefore, table 6.10 calculates the salaries relative to both the GDP per capita of Sudan (all) and an estimated GDP per capita for South Sudan (as explained in chapter 1). The average annual salary in primary schools (all staff, excluding volunteers) is 4.4 times the estimated South Sudan GDP per capita. But it is 1.6 times the GDP per capita for all of Sudan. The average annual salary in secondary school is 6.3 times the estimated South Sudan GDP per capita, but only 2.3 times the GDP per capita of all of Sudan.

In total, out of an estimated 51,000 education sector staff working in the states, some 20,000 are volunteers. Until this point, the analysis has focused on the staff included on the payroll. When we compare payroll

Figure 6.5   Illustration of Categories of Staff Included in the Payroll versus the EMIS Databases, 2009

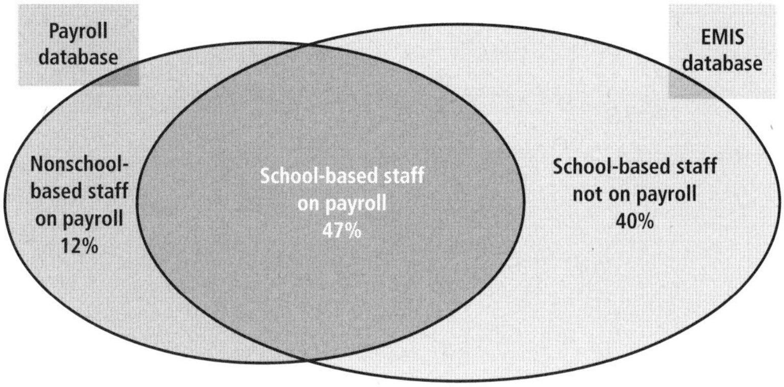

Payroll database

EMIS database

Nonschool-based staff on payroll 12%

School-based staff on payroll 47%

School-based staff not on payroll 40%

Source: Estimation based on analysis of the payroll and EMIS databases.

data with EMIS, we find that EMIS includes some 20,000 volunteers who work in schools but are not on payroll. This gives a total education staff working in the states of about 51,000 (30,616 paid and 20,000 unpaid).[7]

Figure 6.5 illustrates all the educational staff in the states—and the coverage of the two databases with information about staff. The figure shows that 12 percent are nonschool-based staff on payroll (mainly educational officials and administrative staff at state educational offices), some 47 percent are school-based staff on payroll (mainly teachers and administrative staff at school), and another 40 percent are school-based staff who are not on payroll (volunteer teachers and other volunteers in the schools). This serves to illustrate the very large number of persons working in schools on a volunteer basis.

PUBLIC PER STUDENT SPENDING IN 2009

Table 6.11 calculates the public per student spending in primary and secondary schools by dividing total public recurrent spending with enrollments at these two levels (in public schools). The per student spending is SDG 118 in primary education, SDG 349 in secondary education, and SDG 2,183 in higher education in 2009. Public spending per student in secondary education is three times higher than in primary schools. Secondary schools are more expensive to run because of the need for more specialized teachers, laboratories, and so forth. Public spending per student in higher education is 18 times higher than in primary schools. This substantial difference may reflect that the universities are fairly small and

Table 6.11 Public per Student Spending by Level of Education, 2009

Education level	Per student salary spending		Per student operating spending	Total per student spending	
	School-based staff	Nonschool-based staff		SDG	Multiples of primary
Primary	67 (57%)	26 (22%)	25 (21%)	118	1
Secondary	181 (52%)	94 (27%)	74 (21%)	349	3
Higher education	1,555 (71%)		628 (29%)	2,183	19
Memo item: Higher education (including from own revenues[a])	2,023 (73%)		759 (27%)	2,782	24

Source: World Bank estimation.
Note: a. This unit cost includes spending from all the universities' revenues, including own revenues from student fees.

have little economy of scale. Also, the higher cost may reflect higher costs in northern Sudan, where most students are enrolled, and the additional costs of maintaining campuses in both northern Sudan and the Republic of South Sudan. In general, per student spending gives a picture of the allocations of public resources to the average student attending each level. Following the level of per student spending and changes in its composition over time is particularly useful for monitoring the use of resources within the education system. Per student spending data are also useful for making projections of future resource needs.

In primary education, 57 percent of the per student spending goes to salaries paid to staff working in schools and another 22 percent to salaries paid to staff that do not work in school; 21 percent is for operating expenses, most of which are at central MoE level. In secondary education, the percentages are quite similar. In higher education, a higher share of spending goes to nonsalary spending (29 percent) compared with primary and secondary education because of the social subsidy to support students' living costs.

Table 6.12 calculates the average per student spending for primary schools in each state. It is not surprising that there is considerable variation in the primary per student spending across states. This variation is consistent with two of the earlier findings of this chapter: (a) staff are not distributed across the states proportional to enrollments, and (b) there are differences in the average salary of primary school staff across states. Primary per student spending in Upper Nile is only SDG 35, compared with SDG 259 in Western Bahr Ghazal.

At the secondary school level, there are also large disparities across states in per student spending (table 6.13). Per student spending varies between SDG 98 in Lakes and SDG 740 in Western Bahr Ghazal, according to table 6.13. The 10 National Secondary schools—also included in

Table 6.12 Decomposition of Primary School per Student Spending by State, 2009

| State | Salary (SDG) | | Opera-ting cost (SDG) | Per student spending, total (SDG) | Salary (%) | | Opera-ting cost (%) | Total (%) |
	School based	Nonschool based			School based	Nonschool based		
Central Equatoria	80	27	29	136	59	20	21	100
Eastern Equatoria	107	23	35	165	65	14	21	100
Jonglei	50	19	18	87	57	22	21	100
Lakes	77	28	29	134	58	21	21	100
Northern Bahr Ghazal	72	31	28	132	55	24	21	100
Unity	126	32	42	200	63	16	21	100
Upper Nile	18	10	7	35	51	28	21	100
Warrap	77	36	30	143	54	25	21	100
Western Bahr Ghazal	115	89	55	259	44	34	21	100
Western Equatoria	54	25	21	100	54	25	21	100
Weighted average	67	26	25	118	57	22	21	100

Source: World Bank estimation.

Table 6.13 Decomposition of Secondary Education per Student Spending by State, 2009

| State | Salary (SDG) | | Opera-ting cost (SDG) | Per student spending, total (SDG) | Salary (%) | | Opera-ting cost (%) | Total (%) |
	School based	Nonschool based			School based	Nonschool based		
Central Equatoria	128	44	46	217	59	20	21	100
Eastern Equatoria	340	73	111	524	65	14	21	100
Jonglei	420	158	156	734	57	22	21	100
Lakes	56	21	21	98	58	21	21	100
Northern Bahr Ghazal	181	79	70	330	55	24	21	100
Unity	254	63	85	402	63	16	21	100
Upper Nile	146	82	62	290	51	28	21	100
Warrap	148	70	58	277	54	25	21	100
Western Bahr Ghazal	329	254	157	740	44	34	21	100
Western Equatoria	287	132	112	532	54	25	21	100
Weighted average	652	32	181	865	75	4	21	100

Source: World Bank estimation.

the table—have an even higher per student spending of SDG 865. These are considered elite secondary schools, so the higher per student spending is perhaps not surprising.

INTERNATIONAL COMPARISON OF PER STUDENT SPENDING

For the purpose of international comparability, per student spending is usually expressed as percentage of the country's GDP per capita. Using the South Sudan GDP per capita estimate, the per student cost is 11 percent of GDP per capita in primary education and 31 percent in secondary education (this is calculated by dividing the per student cost by the GDP per capita).

Table 6.14 compares these values with the level of per student spending (expressed as a percentage of GDP per capita) with selected countries. As before, two sets of values are shown for South Sudan, since the choice of which GDP per capita to use is not obvious.

Table 6.14   International Comparison of Public per Student Spending as Percentage of per Capita GDP, by Level of Education, LAY

State	Primary (% of GDP/capita)	Secondary (% of GDP/capita)	Higher (% of GDP/capita)	(in US$)
The Republic of South Sudan using all Sudan GDP/capita	4	11	69	973
The Republic of South Sudan using RoSS GDP/capita estimate	11	31	196	973
Northern Sudan	8	24	48	673
Neighboring countries in SSA				
Central African Republic	9	28	305	1,035
Chad	10	28	295	1,652
Ethiopia	11	13	643	1,009
Kenya	22	22	273	1,495
Uganda	11	27	121	367
Average neighboring countries	**13**	**24**	**327**	**1,112**
Lower-middle-income countries in MENA				
Jordan	14	17	—	—
Morocco	20	38	72	1,234
Tunisia	22	24	54	1,544
Average MENA countries	**19**	**26**	**63**	**1,389**

Source: World Bank estimation. World Bank EdStats.
Note: LAY = latest available year; MENA = Middle East and North Africa; RoSS = the Republic of South Sudan; SSA = Sub-Saharan Africa. — = not available.

Primary per student spending in South Sudan (11 percent) is similar to the level of spending of most of the low-income SSA countries shown (for which, the average is 13 percent), but lower than the levels observed in all the three lower-middle-income MENA countries (average of 19 percent), if the South Sudan GDP per capita estimate is used. The opposite is the case for secondary education, where per student spending in South Sudan (31 percent) is higher than the two other country group averages (24 percent in low-income SSA and 26 percent in lower-middle-income MENA). However, the secondary cycle in South Sudan is more comparable to upper secondary education for purposes of international comparisons, and upper secondary usually has higher per student spending than lower secondary (Majgaard and Mingat 2012).

In higher education, the per student spending (when expressed as a share of GDP per capita) is in the lower part of the range observed in the five SSA countries but considerably higher than in all three MENA countries. For an added perspective, the table also shows the higher education per student spending expressed in U.S. dollars. This indicator is strikingly similar in most of the countries shown (except Uganda), an indication that the cost of providing higher education, in particular the cost of academic staff, is largely determined in a regional (labor) market rather than national. Expressed in U.S. dollars, the public per student spending in South Sudan is US$973.

If we base the comparisons on the GDP per capita of all of Sudan, per student spending levels appear very low compared with those of the comparator countries.

HOUSEHOLD SPENDING ON EDUCATION

Although South Sudan has a policy of fee-free primary education, some fees likely remain. One state reported charging SDG 10 for registration of children in primary school (and SDG 35 for secondary school) but also said that fees were lower in rural areas than in urban. The justification for registration fees is often that they are needed to pay for materials. The large number of volunteers in schools might also be receiving some support from parents and communities to sustain their livelihoods; or perhaps a portion of the registration fee goes to the volunteers. It seems no fees are charged for AES. More information is needed on school fees and their use, and on the financial arrangements for the volunteers.

Although not conclusive, household survey data indicate moderate levels of household spending on basic education. The most recent household survey, NBHS 2009, offers some evidence of the magnitude of household education spending. Table 6.15 shows per student household

Table 6.15 Household Education Spending by Level of Education, Total and per Student, 2009

Education level	Aggregate household spending in a year (SDG)	Average per student (SDG)
Primary	2,275,597	1.6
Secondary	770,167	5.0
Higher	215,036	7.0
Not currently enrolled (for ages 6–30)	2,162,187	2.6
Subtotal general education	5,422,988	2.3
Vocational	114,868,627	798.5
Total	120,291,615	47.3

Source: Analysis of NBHS 2009.

spending by level of education. On average, parents reported spending SDG 1.6 per primary school student and SDG 5.0 per secondary school student per year. They spent only a little more, SDG 7.0, on higher education students but a lot on vocational training.[8] Parents also reported spending on the children who were not enrolled (SDG 2.6), suggesting that parents may pay for tutoring or other nonformal arrangements for those children. The aggregate household spending on education in 2009, according to the household survey, was SDG 120.3 million. This is equivalent to about half of GoRSS's education spending in 2009. Most of the household spending went to vocational training (adolescents and adults), however, and not to basic education.

KEY FINDINGS

- **Due to a budgetary crisis, public education spending declined in real terms after its 2008 peak and is now lower than when the Comprehensive Peace Agreement (CPA) was established.** Since the school-age population is growing every year, this has led to a decline in public education spending per child. The sector receives between 5 and 8 percent of total GoRSS spending, a share that has remained more or less stable over the years.
- The primary cycle as a whole receives 55 percent of public recurrent education spending. **Thus, the budget allocation to the first six years**

of primary education is approximately 45–50 percent, a level comparable to other countries in the region. Secondary education receives 18 percent and higher education 19 percent, when GoNU's financing is included.

- Salaries constitute the largest spending component, on average, 77 percent of total GoRSS education spending (or 79 percent of recurrent spending). **There are about 51,000 education staff working in the 10 states; only 30,616 of these are on payroll, while some 20,000 are volunteers.**

- The 10 states are the employers of the frontline staff and are therefore responsible for managing most of the public education spending. There are wide disparities in the resources available to the states, however. For example, **staff are not distributed across the states consistent with enrollments, and it seems states are able to pay widely different average salaries with the resources they receive.** The end result is widely different levels of average per student spending in both primary and secondary schools. Thus, there is considerable scope for improving the distribution of staff and resources across the states to enable a more geographically equitable development of the education system.

- **Public per student spending is SDG 118 in primary school, SDG 349 in secondary school, and SDG 1,555 in higher education, on average.** The primary per student spending, which corresponds to about 11 percent of GDP per capita, is comparable to the level of spending observed in other SSA countries that are at a similar level of income.[9]

- **There are still primary school fees in some states**, but not much is known about fees, or about whether parents are funding the many volunteer teachers. In the most recent household survey, parents reported fairly moderate amounts of yearly education spending. More information is needed to determine whether school fees are limiting access to school for some children.

NOTES

1. With a few exceptions as discussed later in this chapter, the mobile AES centers and 10 National Secondary Schools are funded directly from MoE's budget.

2. These data are sourced from a workshop in Juba in February 2010, in which the director generals of the state ministries of education (SMoEs) of a number of states participated.

3. Arapi TTI, Maridi TTI, and Aramweer TTI.

4. Maridi Department of Curriculum Development Center, Printing Press, and Institute of National Languages.

5. This is a time-consuming process and the result includes some degree of error, since school names may not always reflect the levels of education actually taught in the school.

6. Appendix E includes more detailed tables showing the composition of recurrent spending in each state, by level of education.

7. These figures exclude staff working in MoE.

8. It is difficult to interpret the high levels of spending on vocational training reported in the household survey.

9. When an estimated GDP per capita for Republic of South Sudan is used.

CHAPTER 7

Teachers and Teacher Management

The education sector in the Republic of South Sudan has the highest number of civil servants, similar to other countries. Within the sector, teachers constitute the largest number of employees and the most geographically dispersed. This chapter focuses on the recruitment and management of teachers to provide quality education in South Sudan. Providing quality education is dependent on the timeliness and effectiveness of instruction in classrooms.

Building an adequately sized and competent teaching force presented a much greater challenge for the education system in South Sudan when compared to other countries. First, at the end of the 20-year conflict, the employee database was not up-to-date. Accurate information on how many teachers actually taught in the 10 states was needed to estimate resource requirements. Second, there was no information on the academic qualification of teachers—how many teachers possessed elementary and secondary certification or a tertiary degree commensurate with grade level responsibilities. Data were also not available on whether teachers had any professional or preservice qualifications such as a diploma or a degree in the field of education. Third, the conflict years halted the establishment of a system of teacher management with the necessary institutions, rules, procedures, and, most important, a system of supervision that included both incentives and sanctions.

This chapter deals with how South Sudan is addressing the three challenges described above, and the implications for continuing to tackle these concerns. The chapter discusses (a) the ongoing task of establishing a teacher workforce; (b) the status and challenges of ensuring that both new teachers and teachers working in the system possess a minimum level of academic and professional qualifications with corresponding remuneration to enable effective instruction; and (c) the elements required for an effective system of teacher management.

ESTABLISHING A TEACHER WORKFORCE

After the Comprehensive Peace Agreement (CPA) was established and government resources became available through the implementation of the oil-sharing agreements, the Government of the Republic of South Sudan (GoRSS) prioritized establishing a civil servant teaching cadre. Goldsmith (2010) describes how government pay has become the principal source of income for the majority of South Sudan's teachers. This signifies a fundamental change from the situation before the CPA, when most schools were run and funded by communities, nongovernmental organizations (NGOs), or churches.

In early 2008, the Ministry of Education, Science and Technology (MoEST) conducted a field headcount of teachers to identify and gather basic data on teachers, including grade, work station, and qualifications. Those conduction the headcount visited schools, where each teacher would fill in a form under supervision from an enumerator and then countersigned by the school's head teacher. It was decided not to include other school-based staff in the headcount. The headcount gave a "sighting shot" of teachers and has been the basis for resource allocation between states. As of 2008, the Education Management Information System (EMIS) has also been collecting data on teachers, and efforts are ongoing to compare and integrate the two (Goldsmith 2010).

The headcount process helped focus resources on frontline staff by providing greater visibility to the use of resources. The process included retrenchment of unproductive or nonteaching staff, thereby giving room to hire more teachers, including some who used to be volunteers. It has also helped make progress toward harmonizing salary grades across states, although more work needs to be done in this area, as discussed later.

TEACHER PAYROLL

After the headcount, MoEST commissioned the implementation of a basic computerized payroll system in the states. Under the leadership of the MoEST Payroll Unit, the payroll system was implemented in most states between October 2008 and December 2009. Table 7.1 presents the implementation progress as of January 2010 and describes the specific accomplishments in each state. The payroll system allows state ministries of education (SMoEs) to calculate and prepare pay slips or pay sheets for

Table 7.1 Status of Payroll System Implementation in the 10 States

State	Payroll actions and status
Central Equatoria	SMoE was pressed by MoEST to address, through downsizing, the issue of chronic arrears arising from massive overcommitment: downsizing of over 1,000 least productive staff in 2010.
Eastern Equatoria	More than 500 new teachers recruited and paid by SMoE in 2009 with funds saved from better management and availability of information allowing for the retrenchment of unproductive staff.
Jonglei	SMoE is in the process of reconciling legacy payroll data with EMIS data to improve payroll system.
Lakes	SMoE has brought its grading into line with the rest of the country. This ended the practice of unsustainably high grading, which had entailed payment on rotation.
Northern Bahr Ghazal	System introduction exposed nonstandard pay and deductions.
Unity	SMoE retrenched almost 350 unclassified staff in May 2010. System visibility to GoRSS has given SMoE a much stronger hand to play with the State Ministry of Finance over delays or withholding of payment.
Upper Nile	GoRSS has won a long-standing dispute with the State Ministry of Finance and secured agreement that control of health and education pay will be released back to the line ministries. In addition, GoRSS secured a switch over to standard GoRSS pay scales.
Warrap	The State Minister of Education has used the newly established system of payroll as an opportunity to run a full screening of teachers in person.
Western Bahr Ghazal	The state retrenched more than 700 unproductive staff; teachers in former liberated areas are receiving in some cases 150 percent more pay, now that they have moved to the standard GoRSS pay scales. Pay has moved up from 65 percent to 70 percent of mandated basic pay in 2010, and will go up again once further retrenchment is carried out.
Western Equatoria	Introduction of the system enabled MoEST and GoRSS to press SMoE on retrenchment of a large raft of supernumerary unclassified staff.

Source: Booz & Company 2010.

disbursing salaries. SMoEs submit these paylists to GoRSS for the release of funds for teacher pay. SMoEs disburse salaries to teachers; salaries are paid in cash, usually at schools, but sometimes at the *payam* or county offices. The new payroll system has made it easier for teachers to collect their pay, thereby reducing teacher absences.

TEACHER WORKFORCE AND SALARY GRADES

There are about 25,000 teachers in primary schools and 1,700 teachers in secondary schools across South Sudan. One of the most striking features of the teacher workforce is the low share of female teachers. On the whole, 13 percent of primary school teachers and 11 percent of secondary school teachers are female, but there is considerable variation across states (table 7.2). Presently, women make up 24 percent of enrollments in the primary teacher training colleges, so the share of female teachers is only set to increase slowly.

South Sudan is establishing a classification of teachers into 14 salary grades. Though grades 13 and 14 are supposed to be support staff and may not be qualified, there are persons in these grades teaching in schools in South Sudan (figure 7.1). Four percent of teachers in primary and 18 percent of teachers in secondary are not classified (grade level 0). It is likely that there are difficulties in classifying these teachers in one of the salary grades or this group of teachers is in private schools. Private schools pay their own teachers, and the estimated number for this group is about 2,000 (Goldsmith 2010). About 34 percent of teachers are in grade 14 in primary and 9 percent in secondary schools. Thirty-six percent are in grade 20 in primary and 11 percent in secondary schools. This indicates that more than a third of the teachers in primary are not paid. Moreover, there are few teachers in the higher salary grades. In spite of ongoing efforts to appoint teachers to appropriate salary grades based on experience, qualifications, and performance, this will take a few more years to achieve.[1]

Table 7.2   Share of Female Teachers in Primary and Secondary Schools, 2009

State	Female teachers in primary (%)	Female teachers in secondary (%)
Central Equatoria	21	15
Eastern Equatoria	13	10
Western Equatoria	14	8
Jonglei	8	8
Unity	8	13
Upper Nile	21	14
Lakes	8	7
Warrap	7	4
Western Bahr Ghazal	23	9
Northern Bahr Ghazal	8	8
The Republic of South Sudan	13	11

Source: Analysis of EMIS 2009.

Figure 7.1 Distribution of Teachers by Salary Grade, 2009

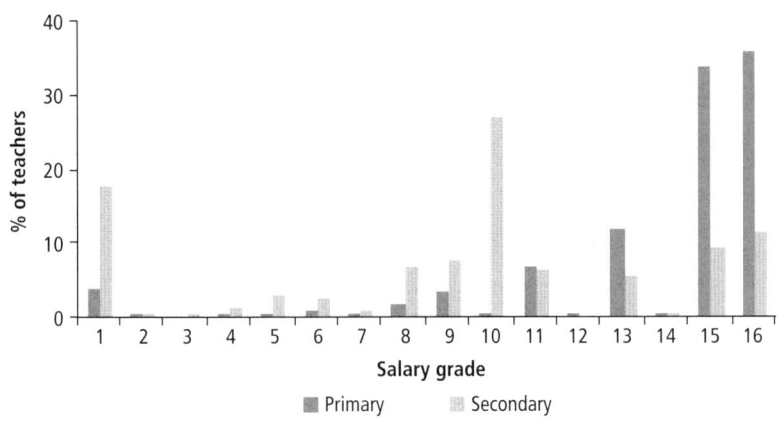

Source: Analysis of EMIS 2010.

Paying teachers in a way that is consistent with their experience and qualifications continues to be a challenge. Since complete data on teachers' years of service are not available, qualifications play a greater role in allocating teachers to a particular salary grade. Though there is no record of the length of service prior to the CPA, it is likely that estimates of this dimension inform decisions on salaries. This would especially apply to those individuals recruited during the war without prior qualifications. Moreover, it is likely that ad hoc pay increases to teachers have taken place since clear policies associated with this area were only introduced recently. Correspondence between qualifications, experience, and pay scales in South Sudan will take time to accomplish.

TEACHER PREPARATION AND QUALIFICATIONS

The academic and professional qualifications of teachers determine the quality of instruction in the classroom. The subject-content knowledge of primary school teachers is weak. As part of the Service Delivery Study (SDS) in the four states, a subsample of 160 teachers took the same mathematics and language tests that were given to students. The mean score for teachers (figure 7.2) in mathematics is 63 percent and in language 62 percent. Only about 28 percent of teachers in mathematics and 31 percent of teachers in language obtained a score of 80 percent and above. These levels reflect teachers' limited mastery of the curriculum that they must teach. Teachers' content knowledge exhibited in these assessments indicates the critical need for developing both the preservice and in-service training of teachers.

Figure 7.2   Teacher Performance in Mathematics and Language in Four States, 2010

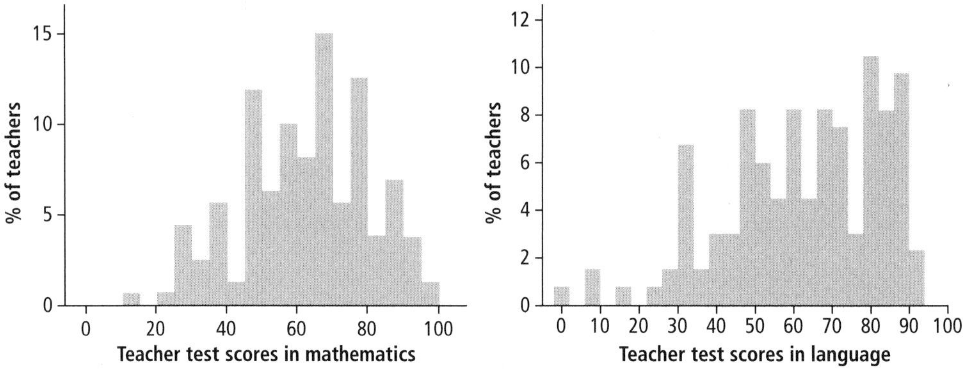

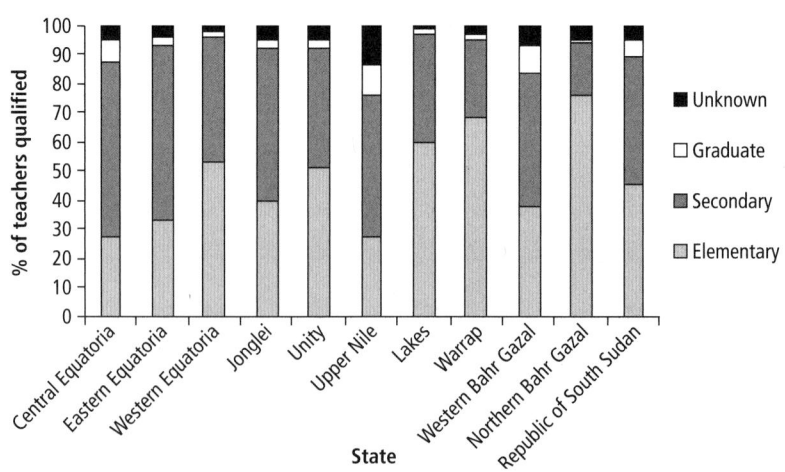

Source: Analysis of SDS 2010.

QUALIFICATION OF TEACHERS

South Sudan does not have enough academically qualified teachers, especially in primary schools. In primary schools, overall, 46 percent of teachers have just primary school education and 45 percent have secondary certification. States such as Lakes, Northern Bahr Ghazal, and Warrap have the highest percentage of teachers with only a primary school certificate (figure 7.3). In Central and Eastern Equatoria and Jonglei states, more than 50 percent of teachers have a secondary certificate. It will be important for the group of teachers with only primary education to upgrade their basic

Figure 7.3   Primary Teachers' Academic Qualifications, 2009

Source: Analysis of EMIS 2009.

Figure 7.4 Secondary Teachers' Academic Background, 2009

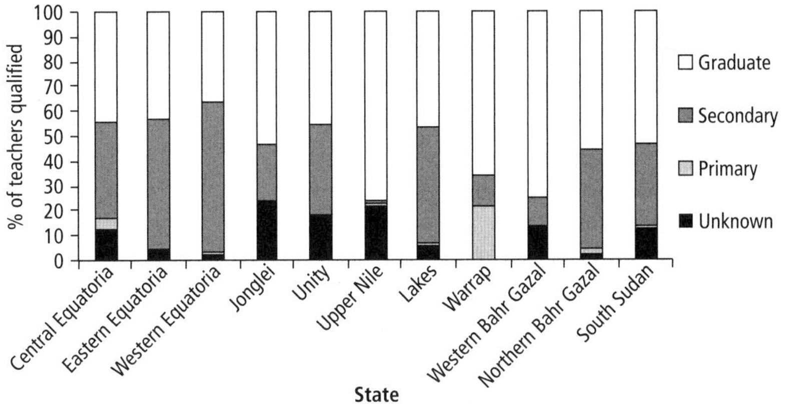

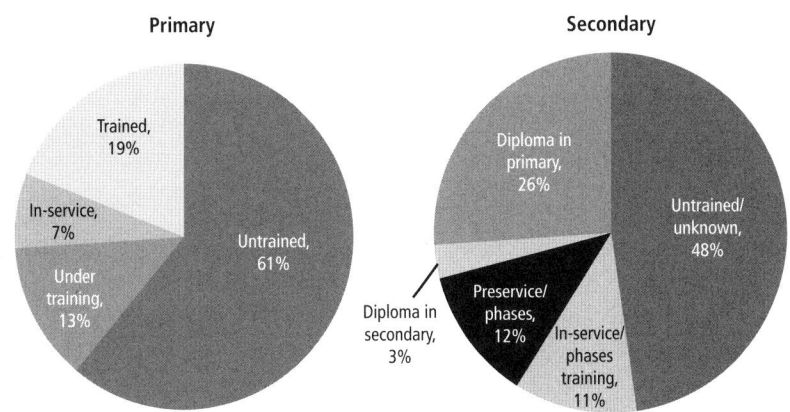

Source: Analysis of EMIS 2009.

academic qualifications. In secondary schools, the situation is better (figure 7.4). Fifty-three percent of teachers are graduates and 33 percent have secondary education. A significant proportion of teachers in states such as Upper Nile, Warrap (77 percent), Western Bahr Ghazal (76 percent), and Warrap (66 percent) possess a graduate degree.

Teachers with professional qualifications are also few in South Sudan. In primary schools, only about 16 percent of teachers are trained and about 61 percent do not possess any preservice training (figure 7.5, left panel). Thirteen percent of teachers are working on their preservice qualifications. In secondary schools, about 48 percent of teachers' profes-

Figure 7.5 Teachers' Professional Qualifications, 2009

Source: Analysis of EMIS 2009.

sional backgrounds are either unknown or limited to a primary certificate (figure 7.5, right panel). Twenty-six percent have only a diploma in primary education. Twelve percent of teachers possess preservice training specific to secondary education and 11 percent have a diploma in secondary education. Three percent are undergoing professional training.

PROFESSIONAL TRAINING OF TEACHERS

According to the United States Agency for International Development (USAID), there are "specific policy and legal issues that need to be harmonized related to the ongoing establishment of teacher training institutions … and the curriculum content of in-service and pre-service programs" (USAID 2009: vi).

After the CPA, the first major intervention of the MoEST to deal with the low levels of both the academic and professional qualifications of primary teachers was to introduce a Fast Track Training Program (FTTP). MoEST completed the design and curriculum for the FTTP at the end of 2006. The six-week course included modules on class preparation, student management, approaches to teaching and learning, teaching methods, and supplementary self-study materials. Modules were adapted to the situation in each state. Over 1,200 teachers have participated in the FTTP. In addition, to the FTTP, several NGOs offered alternative teacher training programs of varying quality and length. Significant among them was the "Distance Teacher Education Program" from the United Nations Children's Fund (UNICEF) and the "Sudan Basic Education Program" from USAID for both academic and professional training.

MoEST has recently developed a "National Teacher Education Strategy," which is multifaceted and includes both preservice and in-service training of teachers working in the school system. The strategy proposed the following institutions for preservice training in primary education: teaching training institutes (TTIs) in each state and two Cluster Education Centers (CECs) in each county. This would amount to 10 TTIs and 158 CECs. Table 7.3 lists proposed and ongoing preservice training programs. In 2009, 2,445 students (USAID 2009) were enrolled in various government and NGO programs to become teachers in primary schools. Of this number, 595 were women.

Preservice training for secondary schools includes a two-year diploma, a four-year graduate degree, and a one-year diploma after an undergraduate degree. Five universities can offer these programs—Bahr El Ghazal, Juba, Rumbek, Upper Nile, and Rumbek. However, only three are functioning—Juba, Upper Nile, and Bahr El Ghazal. In 2009, 2,357 students

Table 7.3 Preservice Programs Organized by GoRSS, 2009

Duration	Prior qualification	Institutions	Qualification
Two-year residential training	Secondary	Teacher training institutes	Primary School Teaching Certificate
Four-year residential training	Primary	Teacher training institutes	Primary School Teaching Certificate
Four-year training (distance learning and face-to-face training for 60 days during school vacations)	Working teachers	Cluster Education Centers	Primary School Teaching Certificate

Source: MoEST 2009.

were enrolled to become teachers in secondary schools. Of this number, only 393 were women.

In-service training is undertaken by both the government and by NGOs. A variety of short courses are offered to address thematic areas such as English speaking and the needs of specific groups such as Arabic trained teachers, returnees, and so forth (table 7.4).

TEACHER MANAGEMENT

This section deals with the evolving system of teacher management in South Sudan. It addresses the status of teacher recruitment, teacher deployment and transfer, and the system in place for the supervision of teacher performance, especially instruction.

Table 7.4 In-service Programs Offered in the Republic of South Sudan, 2009

In-service programs	Participants
Training for alternative learning programs	Teachers without a Primary School Leaving Certificate
Two-month Fast Track Training Program	Teachers
Six-month beginner English training	Arabic and community teachers
Six-month intensive English training	Teachers with secondary education, Arabic and community teachers
Radio instruction (12 weeks) for Accelerated Learning Programme teachers	Sudan Radio Service
Four-week training for trainers of Accelerated Learning Programme teachers	ALP department
Continuing professional development	Teachers

Source: MoEST 2009.

TEACHER RECRUITMENT

According to the teacher recruitment policies articulated by state officials examined in five states, a secondary school diploma is required for teaching in primary education and an undergraduate degree for teaching in secondary schools. No state mentions the need for professional qualifications. Counties are responsible for identifying the number of new teachers required and the state is accountable for managing the recruitment process. After states advertise vacant posts on the radio, prospective candidates collect their application forms from SMoEs. Candidates have to present certificates to confirm qualifications (Sudanese, Ugandan, Kenyan, or any other equivalent), birth, and nationality, in addition to a handwritten application (must be their own writing). States establish a committee to conduct interviews and hire new teachers. Some states maintain detailed minutes of the interviews and decisions made on chosen candidates. The departments that deal with labor and public services in particular are involved with the recruitment of new teachers.

For a variety of reasons, some of them mentioned in table 7.1, states find it difficult to recruit new teachers. State authorities admit that they recruit a significant number of teachers that are not included on payroll as a result of funding constraints. These teachers are either voluntary or informally paid. For example, Torit county in Eastern Equatorial State indicated that 30 new teachers were in schools but were not on payroll. Although states are responsible for hiring teachers, due to the acuteness of need at the school level, principals and parents try to hire teachers. Schools often hire teachers for instruction in primary school with just primary education or secondary school with just secondary school qualifications. Teachers with experience but without the required qualifications would be preferred candidates on this list. Payments to teachers not on payroll or hired locally are ad hoc, depending on the availability of additional funds.

TEACHER DEPLOYMENT AND TRANSFER

South Sudan's stipulated pupil-to-teacher ratio (PTR) is 50:1 for primary and 40:1 for secondary. However, there was no evidence that teacher deployment and transfer actually takes place on the basis of these norms. As shown in table 7.5, average PTRs vary greatly from one state to the next—from 31 students per teacher in Central Equatoria to 84 students per teacher in Jonglei. (If volunteer teachers are excluded from the PTR, the range is from 51 students per teacher in Central Equatoria to 145 students per teacher in Jonglei.) Official descriptions of teacher deployment and transfer policies in both primary and secondary subsectors indicate

Table 7.5 Pupil-Teacher Ratios in Public Primary Schools, with and without Volunteers, 2009

State	Paid teachers only		Including volunteers	
	Pupil-teacher ratio (%)	Number of teachers in average school (E = 425)	Pupil-teacher ratio (%)	Number of teachers in average school (E = 425)
Central Equatoria	51	8	31	14
Eastern Equatoria	82	5	38	11
Jonglei	145	3	84	5
Lakes	65	7	50	8
Northern Bahr Ghazal	86	5	56	8
Unity	102	4	62	7
Upper Nile	131	3	72	6
Warrap	91	5	50	9
Western Bahr Ghazal	61	7	49	9
Western Equatoria	54	8	33	13
The Republic of South Sudan	87	5	52	8

Source: Analysis of EMIS 2009.
Note: The number of teachers in an average school is calculated based on the linear relation between the number of teachers and the number of students in public schools in each state. E = enrollment.

that South Sudan is very much at a nascent stage, requiring policies and procedures to guide its implementation.

In principle, teachers can be transferred within counties (from *payam* to *payam*) and across counties. However, in practice, as no transport or housing is provided, transfers of teachers are rare in primary. According to state officials, teacher transfers take place usually in an ad hoc manner. Sometimes transfers are carried out to balance the number of teachers in a school, provide subject specialist teachers, or as a means of disciplining the teacher. Misbehavior or misconduct warrants a transfer to another county. State officials in Central Equatoria indicate that teachers can be transferred after staying in a school for just one year. In Lakes State, primary teachers remain in their own counties due to security reasons; therefore, the primary responsibility for transfers between schools lies with the county official. Transfers are more prevalent in secondary education. In Western Bahr Ghazal, 9 and 10 teachers were transferred in secondary schools in 2008 and 2009, respectively. Lakes transferred three teachers in 2009.

Figure 7.6 shows a scatterplot of all South Sudan's public primary schools according to their enrollments and number of teachers. The graph also includes a linear regression line, which is the number of teachers expressed as a function of the number of students. The data points are distributed in a

Figure 7.6   Consistency between Number of Teachers and Pupils in Government Primary Schools, 2009

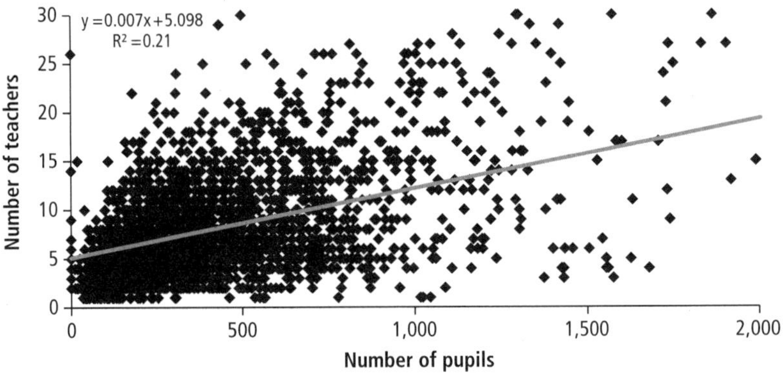

$y = 0.007x + 5.098$
$R^2 = 0.21$

Source: Analysis of EMIS 2009. Each dot or observation represents a school.
Note: Chart is based on government schools only. The number of teachers includes volunteer teachers.

cloud rather than very close to the regression line; this suggests that the number of students in a school is not a good predictor of how many teachers work in the school—that is, the relation between the two is weak (and the R^2, the statistical measure of the strength of this relation, is only 0.21).

Figure 7.7 compares the "degree of randomness" in the primary teacher allocation in South Sudan (calculated as $1 - R^2$, that is, 0.79), with the corresponding values for a large number of Sub-Saharan African

Figure 7.7   International Comparison of Degree of Randomness ($1-R^2$) in Teacher Allocation to Public Primary Schools, 2009

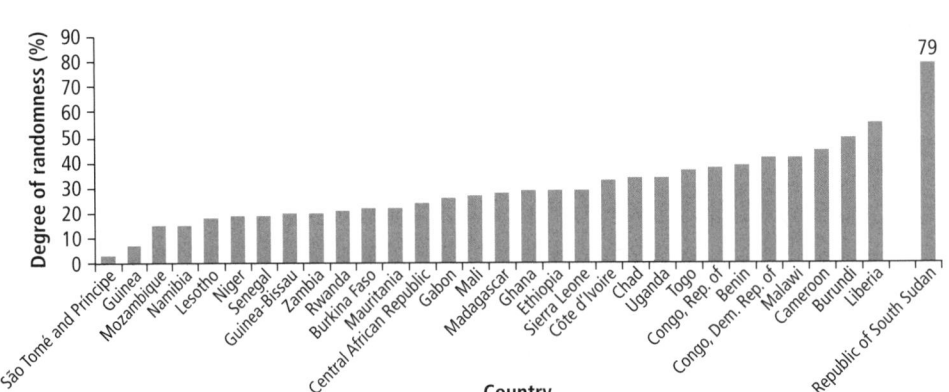

Source: World Bank database.
Note: The graph compares the degree of randomness, which is calculated as $1-R^2$, in the regression between number of teachers as a function of number of students.

Table 7.6 Teacher Deployment: Coefficient of Determination across States, 2009

State	R^2
Central Equatoria	0.59
Eastern Equatoria	0.45
Jonglei	0.17
Lakes	0.34
Northern Bahr Ghazal	0.35
Unity	0.15
Upper Nile	0.09
Warrap	0.30
Western Bahr Ghazal	0.41
Western Equatoria	0.63
The Republic of South Sudan	0.21

Source: Analysis of EMIS 2009.
Note: Table is based on government schools only, but includes volunteer teachers.

countries. As shown, South Sudan has the highest degree of randomness of all the countries shown, which means the weakest and most inconsistent distribution of teachers across schools as a function of enrollments.

When the R^2 is compared across states (table 7.6 and figure 7.8), predictability is highest in Central Equatoria (R^2 0.59) and lowest in Upper Nile (R^2 0.09). This means that Central Equatoria manages teachers quite

Figure 7.8 States with Highest Predictability (Central Equatoria) and Lowest Predictability (Upper Nile) in Teacher Deployment, 2009

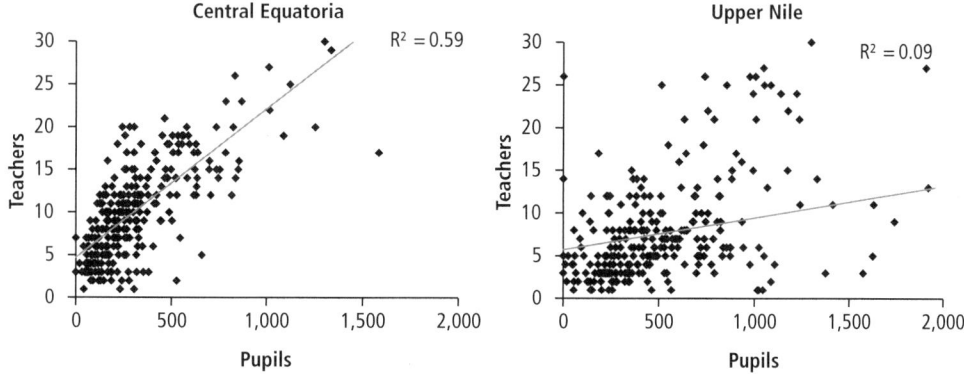

Source: Analysis of EMIS 2009.
Note: Charts are based on government schools only, but include volunteer teachers.

well while teacher management is weak in Upper Nile. Predictability in teacher deployment is weak in South Sudan, partly due to the inability of the system to distribute teachers across counties and schools within a state.

TEACHER SUPERVISION

The SMoE is responsible for the supervision of secondary schools and teacher performance, as well as the county and *payam* offices for primary. Teachers are expected to be supervised three times a year. However, due to a shortage of staff and financial resources, supervision rarely takes place. At the primary level, one inspector per *payam* is expected to supervise all schools in the *payam*. The range of schools in a *payam* varies from a single school to 53 schools (in Western Equatoria). The uneven distribution of schools (table 7.7) across *payams* makes this task challenging. When there are too many schools, it is not effective and when there are too few schools, it is not efficient. The policy of one inspector per *payam* may not be appropriate to provide oversight and the effective management of teachers. Moreover, there are no financial resources earmarked for this task. At the secondary level, although there are a few supervisors, a clear system of teacher and school supervision is not evident.

States indicate that they do use tools or reporting instruments for school and teacher supervision. However, these tools were not available in any of the states included in the Service Delivery Study.

Table 7.7 Distribution of Schools across *Payams* in States, 2009

State	Number of *payams*	Number of schools in a *payam*	
		Lowest	Highest
Central Equatoria	42	1	35
Eastern Equatoria	55	1	21
Jonglei	65	1	20
Lakes	52	1	16
Northern Bahr Ghazal	50	1	17
Unity	57	1	14
Upper Nile	74	1	17
Warrap	45	1	23
Western Bahr Ghazal	16	1	41
Western Equatoria	46	1	53

Source: Analysis of EMIS 2009.

GoRSS is in the process of introducing a uniform format for supervision, which states have not yet implemented. The tool is comprehensive and captures critical areas associated with instruction in classrooms. The tool examines teaching and learning according to the following areas:

- lesson preparation and planning
- use of resources and classroom environment
- the teaching and learning process
- pupils' understanding and attainment
- assessment and record keeping.

The absence of tools and databases suggests that standards for teacher performance are not yet in place across states. In addition to monitoring teacher performance in class, the importance of monitoring regularity in teacher attendance is increasingly becoming critical. Requests to states for policies and regulations associated with teacher leave and absence from schools did not yield any results. The five states examined indicated that teachers take no leave since they have school vacations when they are not in school. In one state, leave policies set in place during the colonial period were presented as the policy (table 7.8). However, there is no sign that states implement these regulations.

KEY FINDINGS

- **Significant strides have been made in establishing a functioning payroll system for teachers**. Remaining challenges include filling the

Table 7.8 Leave Regulations for Government Officials—1975

Type	Length of leave
Ordinary leave	• This regulation does not apply to the staff who benefit from school vacations
Local leave	• Seven days in a year
Sick leave	• Seven days in a year • More than seven days, first six months with full pay; second six months with half pay • More than one year referred to General Medical Commission
Special leave	• Four years leave without pay to accompany spouse • Seven days for trade union work • Pregnancy two weeks before and six weeks after birth with pay; also eligible for sick leave • Forty-five days per year without pay

Source: GoRSS.

information gaps on teacher experience and qualifications and achieving more uniform teacher pay across states. There is concern about the low proportion of female teachers in both primary and secondary education—less than 15 percent.

- Teachers' subject-content knowledge is weak, which reflects the limited academic and professional training received. The number of adequately trained teachers in primary education is low in South Sudan: 46 percent of teachers have only a primary school education and another 45 percent have secondary education. **About 60 percent of teachers do not possess any professional training to be teachers.** Upgrading the subject-content and pedagogical knowledge of teachers presents an urgent task for South Sudan.

- An effectively managed teaching force is critical to regular school functioning and instructional quality. **Currently, teachers are not allocated to schools in a way that is very consistent with schools' student enrollments. Thus, there is room for improvement in the teacher allocation across schools.** Teacher management policies in South Sudan are evolving and will require concerted efforts to develop, pilot, and fine tune. **Implementing clear recruitment, deployment, and transfer policies that can guide and strengthen the teaching force will be critical.** In addition, setting in place a supervision system that monitors teachers' work will also serve to support and sustain good performance.

NOTES

1. The different administrative traditions in the Republic of South Sudan proved to be a challenge to the process of creating a unified salary structure. Traditions included different treatments of basic allowance; formal and informal appointments; and a variety of approaches to pension, allowances, deductions, taxes, and so forth.

CHAPTER 8

Conclusions

The government and the people of the Republic of South Sudan have every reason to be proud of what has been accomplished in the education system since the Comprehensive Peace Agreement (CPA). Among the most important achievements is the remarkable progress in expanding access to schooling (for example, school enrollments doubled between 2005 and 2009). With independence, South Sudan will continue to grow and consolidate the education system—essentially entering a new phase of sector development.

Because South Sudan has been deprived of a functioning education system for many years, it has faced a double challenge: addressing the pent-up demand for formal educational opportunities and coming to terms with the fact that so many citizens of South Sudan will never have a chance to attend formal schools. Entering a second phase of educational development does not mean that these challenges have now been addressed. Increasing the capacity of the system to stem the flow of and address the stock of out-of-school youth still constitutes the number one priority. However, this report points to a new set of challenges that the country's authorities and other education stakeholders also need to address. By prioritizing these "second order" challenges, South Sudan can avoid many of the stubborn problems that have plagued other education systems: unsustainable growth of the sector in financial and institutional terms, diminished quality, and continued inequities of both quality and access.

With the support of its development partners, the Government of the Republic of South Sudan (GoRSS) has embarked on the preparation of an education sector development plan that will guide reform and investments in the education sector in the coming years. Based on the analyses and findings of this report, we present below a series of priorities and considerations that ought to be addressed during the preparation of this plan:

Step up education spending, as education expenditures on the whole are low compared to the needs, and correct inequities in the distribution across states of recurrent expenditures. GoRSS has given due priority to the development of primary education as evidenced by the substantial financial support for primary teacher salaries. However, current levels of spending are inadequate since schools, without sufficient numbers of paid staff, rely on a large number of volunteers. Furthermore, the budget does not support critical nonsalary expenditures, such as for textbooks. Government spending for teacher salaries does not appear to be equitably distributed, as reflected in student unit costs that vary considerably from one state to another. These inequities stem from GoRSS simply taking on salaries of teachers already in the system, since new hiring has been limited. Clear policies on acceptable pupil-teacher ratios (PTRs) and teacher deployment applied across states will be needed to correct allocation patterns and bring about equity in national teacher spending for salaries.

Strengthen the ability of the GoRSS Ministry of Education (MoE) and state ministries of education (SMoEs) to drive reform, and incorporate nonstate providers' contributions into the overall plan for sector development. A new phase of education development must face increasingly complex challenges. To address these challenges and incorporate the lessons learned during the last six years, three sets of actors must effectively carry out their respective roles and responsibilities: (a) the GoRSS MoE; (b) the SMOEs; and (c) nonstate providers of educational services, including nongovernmental organizations (NGOs), churches, contractors, and firms. The provision of services by these three sets of actors will be most effectively located within a nationwide policy and quality assurance framework. Such a framework can steer South Sudan toward its overall education sector objectives.

The distribution of responsibilities between the GoRSS MoE, the SMoEs, and nonstate actors has already been mapped in the constitution of South Sudan. Education service delivery is framed as the political and administrative responsibility of the states. The GoRSS MoE will formulate policies, norms, and standards; ensure coordination; provide advisory services; promote and disseminate innovations; and enforce quality assurance. Furthermore, state actors (MoE and SMoE) can already contract nonstate actors to provide education services (private or community schools—but also teacher training, school construction, and so forth). Therefore, it is particularly urgent to strengthen the capacities of state-level administrators so that they can support the more complex transformations of the education system.

Both the GoRSS MoE and the SMoEs are relatively recent creations, with weak capacity. As discussed above, the SMoEs have been even weaker and thus in many cases the GoRSS MoE has had to support state ministries to a considerable extent. Furthermore, nonstate actors (NGOs, churches, and so forth) traditionally have had considerable freedom to provide educational services, and have been accountable to external partners rather than the community or the state. Transitioning from this baseline (and progress has already been made) will require a phased approach that captures the comparative strengths of both nongovernmental initiatives within the overall state and national strategic plans for the sector.

Keep a strong focus on increasing access and retention in primary education. The primary school gross enrollment rate (GER) for South Sudan is 72 percent[1] and about one million children in the primary school age group are not in school. With so many children still out of school, it is clear that the expansionary phase of the development of the education system is far from completed. Access to the early grades is steadily increasing, but only about a third of children who enroll in grade 1 complete the primary cycle. Achieving universal primary completion (UPC) will mean increasing both access and retention. The weak primary completion rate may be associated with the high number of primary schools not offering the higher grades. Improving completion within primary education will require completing schools, at least up to grade 6. Moreover, only 25 percent of all schools operate in permanent structures. Enabling schools to offer a complete primary cycle and providing permanent school structures and adequate sanitary facilities are critical for expanding access to schooling in South Sudan. In most Sub-Saharan Africa (SSA) countries, policies to expand the supply of fee-free primary education have been successful at getting most children to school. Supply-side policies, however, may not be sufficient to reach the most marginalized, such as children from very poor families. Demand-side interventions will also need to be considered.

Strengthen and expand second-chance literacy training for out-of-school youth. Despite recent achievements, most school-age children are still out of school, and most youth have never been to school. Although some youth are now enrolled as overage students, most youth will never have access to formal schooling or will not return after dropping out. Improving access must cater to overage students in the "catch-up" phase. About 44 percent of primary school pupils are five or more years overage for their grade. Without expanding the existing capacity of the system, a very large number of youth in South Sudan will never receive formal education; another large group will not finish their basic education. The Alternative Education System (AES) is a unique aspect of South Sudan's education system. If the country is successful in achieving UPC, it is necessary for the AES to continue to play a central role in the overall education system. For now and into the foreseeable future, AES will remain the second most important part of the education system. The tremendous stock of out-of-school youth will continue to need educational opportunities that can only be provided by AES. Generally, the AES has gained a good reputation among partners and the population. Further reinforcement of the quality and measurement of outcomes of this part of the education system should be a key pillar of an ongoing government education strategy.

Address inequity across gender, location, and region. Globally, the gap between boys and girls in access and retention is only 13 percent. However, this triples (44 percent in access and 43 percent in retention) when the urban-rural dimension is considered. While gender inequity is a central feature of South Sudan's education system, particularly in the rural areas where more than 80 percent of the population resides, rural boys are also at a disadvantage. In urban areas where the educational coverage is relatively high, gender inequity is diminishing. Building more schools in rural areas closer to children's homes will expand educational opportunities for all rural children, but those who have the most to gain are the girls.

Performance on key educational outcomes also differs across states. Western Equatoria and Upper Nile are some of the high performers, with primary school GERs of 106 percent and 96 percent, respectively. This is much higher than the GERs for Warrap and Eastern Equatoria, which are 50 percent and 46 percent, respectively. Similar differences are evident with regard to completion rates. Targeted and additional national-level financing and administrative support for the weaker states will be crucial to ensure they can close the gap with the better performing states. Educational systems in the weaker states will require a range of interventions such as improved infrastructure, more teachers, and sufficient instructional material.

Address teacher workforce issues and put in place a system of teacher management. The PTRs of Western Equatoria (51:1) and Central Equatoria (54:1) (only counting paid teachers) are comparable to averages found in most SSA countries. However, the PTR is considerably higher in most other states of the Republic of South Sudan. Even when volunteer teachers are included, the PTR in Jonglei is still high at 84:1. States with high PTRs typically have lower GERs than average, and thus PTRs will only continue to rise over the next few years as more children enter school. Increasing the number of teachers will be critical for the states with more out-of-school children.

Almost half of the teachers in South Sudan are not on the payroll. Little is known about these "volunteer" teachers—as they are referred to in South Sudan—in terms of how they are recruited, paid, trained, or supervised. The GoRSS has not yet established a strategy for the future of volunteer teachers. In reality, most states gradually incorporate them into the payroll. Any strategy must consider the short-, medium-, and long-term budgetary consequences of changing the professional status of these teachers.

Reduce the inequitable deployment of teachers and allocation of textbooks. The historical legacy of "laissez faire" recruitment and deployment undertaken by states before the CPA has led to an uneven deployment of government-paid teachers in South Sudan. The "sighting" system that identified the exact number of teachers in each state marks the beginning of a new approach to address inequities. Correction of the uneven deployment through new policies and practices that are driven by equity will be a crucial task for GoRSS in the years to come.

Textbook procurement and distribution is not yet high on the agenda of GoRSS or state governments due to competing demands. All students need a set of textbooks if the quality of education is to be improved. Therefore, South Sudan needs to establish a sustainable and cost-efficient system of textbook production and distribution.

Focus on improving learning achievement. Low quality of education in South Sudan is not surprising, considering the state of the education system at the time of the CPA. With the government racing to meet demand for schooling, quality may have been temporarily sacrificed. However, delaying improvements in quality is a fundamental error committed by many countries as they expand their education system. This misstep has proven to be very difficult to reverse.

The Service Delivery Study administered standardized language and mathematics learning achievement tests to primary students in Central Equatoria, Lakes, Upper Nile, and Western Bahr Ghazal. The average student test scores were extremely weak. The same test was administered to 160 teachers across the four states and revealed that the knowledge and pedagogical expertise of teachers are acutely limited. These poor results may in part be attributed to the qualifications of teachers. Almost half of teachers have only primary school education and about 60 percent have not received any teacher training. Upgrading the subject matter and pedagogical knowledge of teachers presents an urgent task for South Sudan.

Improve service delivery and school management. Primary schools in South Sudan tend to be overcrowded, and class sizes are large. Between 2002 and 2009, the average enrollment in a primary school doubled to

429 students, resulting in many overcrowded schools. By 2009, schools had an average of 129 pupils per classroom and 52 students per teacher, when volunteers are included. High average class size makes regular instruction difficult to implement. Most of the primary schools (75 percent) and some of the secondary schools (22 percent) do not have permanent structures, which leads to the loss of school working days during inclement weather.

There is a shortage of textbooks, paper, and writing instruments in South Sudan's schools, especially in primary schools, which have an average of one textbook for every three students in both mathematics and English. Two-thirds of students surveyed in the Service Delivery Study did not have paper to write on, and one-fifth of the students did not have pens or other writing instruments. These shortages limit opportunities for reinforcing what is taught.

There are indications that parents and local communities support education. However, schools and teachers are not well managed. Parent-teacher associations (PTAs) were evident in most schools surveyed in the Service Delivery Study. Schools typically also received some financial and in-kind support from local NGOs and communities. However, considerable variation across states is evident in the number of working days in a school year, with some schools functioning for less than eight months a year. The lack of clarity in the number of working days is compounded by the irregularity in the time classes spend on actual instruction. The majority of teachers interviewed in the Service Delivery Study taught for less than 10 hours a week. The deficiencies in working days and instructional hours are reflected in the low syllabus coverage in classrooms.

In addition, the management of schools is weak: few head teachers maintain records on student enrollment, student performance, and teachers' leave. South Sudan has yet to put in place a system of teacher supervision that can provide consistent evaluations of teacher performance. Such a system would include links between teacher performance and pay and the organization of timely and relevant in-service training.

Although more analysis is needed to fully understand education quality, the factors discussed above appear to be the principal contributors to low levels of achievement.

Invest in skills development and post-basic education for the labor market and economic growth. The great influx of children into schools will have a tremendous positive impact on social and economic conditions in South Sudan, but this effect will take some time. The adult population today is characterized by illiteracy or unfinished primary education, and will continue to be so for the foreseeable future.

The demand for high-level skills in the formal labor market is miniscule, and future jobs (primarily construction, roads, and so forth) will probably require mostly low-level skills. However, if the profile of the teacher corps is any indication, it appears that the few jobs that require secondary and tertiary education are not easy to fill. Also, many mid-level technicians, managers, administrators, accountants, and foremen in South Sudan are not Sudanese, but come from places like Kenya, Ethiopia, and Eritrea. Many employers—in the private sector as well as NGOs and bilateral and international agencies—complain about the lack of workers from South Sudan with mid- or high-level skills. Workers who cannot be locally sourced include foremen, accountants, managers, administrators, statisticians, analysts, translators, and teacher trainers.

On the supply side, as noted above, secondary education and tertiary education have relatively low levels of enrollment compared to neighboring countries. This should change as more youth complete primary education and seek opportunities for secondary and higher education. The potential influx to South Sudan of young adults enrolled in the Khartoum campuses may also change this equation, although weak English skills may hamper their potential insertion into the labor force as qualified workers.

The immediate problem is that the existing post-basic education system cannot produce mid-level professionals that are critical for the development of state and nonstate administrative and technical apparatus. Existing higher education is organized in a traditional manner (with, for example, four-year bachelor's degree programs in broad disciplinary areas), and this report found no programs targeted for the development of mid-level technical, administrative, and managerial skills.

Strengthen the capacity for monitoring and evaluation and avoid developing plans that will outstrip implementation capacity or available financial resources. The future development of the education sector in South Sudan will require greater accountability at all levels, which in turn means better and more widely available information about sector trends. It is evident that if policies are to be effectively developed and implemented, much more reliable and detailed data will be needed to measure results and hold state- and national-level administrations accountable. Reliable and detailed data on educational outcomes, deployment of teachers, availability of textbooks, and teacher and school management are needed to measure progress.

The CPA period constituted a first phase of educational development. Now South Sudan enters a second phase, where further expansion must address additional considerations of equity, efficiency, and learning. Building an additional classroom or hiring another teacher may only move South Sudan closer to its education sector objectives if combined with more targeted and effective use of resources. There are many indications that addressing the challenges in the education sector will outstrip strategic and administrative management capacities. This includes capacities for effective monitoring, planning, and quality assurance, as well as the capacity to create proper incentives and meaningful social accountability mechanisms.[2] Options for development need to be considered in tandem with their fiscal implications so that new directions for the sector are financially sustainable. Finally, the next phase of development will require different approaches than under the CPA, because the context has changed with independence and the goals to be attained will require more elaborate solutions.

NOTES

1. The GER is 72 percent for the eight-year primary cycle and 88 percent for the first six years of primary education.

2. This "capacity" consists of technical competence and accountability mechanisms.

Appendixes

APPENDIX A: DATA SOURCES

Chapter 5 uses relevant government documents and reports in addition to recently completed studies in primary and secondary education in the Republic of South Sudan. The main studies that inform this chapter are as follows:

- UNICEF report (2009) entitled *Socio Economic and Cultural Barriers to Schooling in South Sudan.* This study was conducted in the capital cities of three states—Lakes, Upper Nile, and Western Bahr Ghazal. Using qualitative and quantitative methods, the analysis focuses on the context of schooling in selected counties. The study includes interviews and focus group discussions with state, county, *payam*, and school personnel, in addition to a questionnaire administered to 1,195 households.

- Surveys done by the International Organization for Migration (IOM 2009a, 2009b, and 2009c) in three states—Northern Bahr Ghazal, Unity, and Warrap.[1] The surveys include group discussions, individual interviews, observations, and the completion of a village assessment form. The sample included 1,738 villages in Northern Bahr Ghazal, 1,785 villages in Unity, and 2,049 villages in Warrap.

- A 2010 Ministry of Education Service Delivery Study (SDS) done in four states: Central Equatoria, Upper Nile, Western Bahr Ghazal, and Lakes. These states are representative of the major regions in South Sudan. Central Equatoria represents the Equatoria region; Upper Nile, the northern region; Western Bahr Ghazal, the Bahr Ghazal region; and Lakes, the Central region. A random sample of counties, *payams,* and schools in the four states was identified to participate in this study. However, due to security issues, inhospitable terrains, and challenging weather conditions, researchers were unable to ensure the randomness of the sample. While in the states, the research teams were forced to substitute counties and schools in the sample with those that were accessible and safe. This resulted in a convenience sample, with most of the schools located in urban areas. Data from predominantly urban schools are likely to underestimate the gravity of the situation of service delivery and learning outcomes in the average school.

The Service Delivery Study included questionnaires, observation, and student assessment tests in language and mathematics.[2] The sample (table A.1), representing an average of 10 percent of schools in each state, consisted of 40 schools in Central Equatoria, 28 in Lakes, 24 in Upper Nile, and 15 in Western Bahr Ghazal. The head teacher and one or two

Table A.1 Sample Schools for the Service Delivery Study

Basic education (public schools)		Central Equatoria	Lakes	Upper Nile	Western Bahr Ghazal	Total sampled
Number of schools visited	Total	431	281	289	128	1,129
	Sampled	40	28	24	15	107
	Sampled % of total	9.3	10.0	8.3	11.7	9.5
Classrooms observed		123	84	72	41	320
Number of teachers interviewed and tested	Total	4,306	2,211	2,388	1,104	10,009
	Sampled	40	56	50	33	179
	Sampled % of total	0.9	2.5	2.1	3.0	1.8
Number of pupils tested	Total	138,934	110,315	202,425	52,990	504,664
	Sampled	693	433	424	271	1,821
	Sampled % of total	0.5	0.4	0.2	0.5	0.4

Source: Analysis of SDS 2010 and EMIS 2009.

teachers (mathematics and/or language teachers) from each school (a total of 179 teachers) were interviewed using questionnaires. In addition, enumerators observed a grade 3, 4, and 5 class in each school (a total of 320 classes). Twenty randomly selected grade 6 students from each school (1,821 students) took a mathematics and language test. The section on student learning below describes the tests in more detail. Teachers interviewed also completed the same learning assessment tests administered to students.

The analysis provided in the teacher management chapter (chapter 7) uses EMIS data, government and donor documentation and studies, and case studies done in five states on teacher management. The case studies were done at the same time as the Service Delivery Study, in the same four states (Central Equatoria, Upper Nile, Lakes, and Western Bahr Ghazal). The instruments used to collect data included a detailed set of questions for state and county officials related to different aspects of teacher management. Later, the same instruments were also used to collect data in Eastern Equatoria.

NOTES

1. The IOM gathered information on the availability and accessibility of basic infrastructure concerning water and sanitation, health, and education. IOM identified villages using the Global Positioning System (GPS).

2. The South Sudan Multi-Donor Trust Fund (education), administered by the World Bank, financed the Service Delivery Study. Juba University organized and led the data collection in the four states, while the Southern Sudan Centre for Census, Statistics and Evaluation (SSCCSE) was responsible for data entry and collation. The World Bank provided technical assistance. The same study was carried out in northern Sudan for their Education Status Report.

APPENDIX B: SCHOOL-AGE POPULATION IN THE REPUBLIC OF SOUTH SUDAN, 2000–09

METHODOLOGY FOR SMOOTHING POPULATION DATA

For the purpose of this report, the population data for the 2–24 age group were smoothed, which simply means redistributed across single ages while holding the total population constant. The smoothing was done at the level of Sudan's 25 states and then aggregated to national-level data. The methodology is explained for Lakes State below (figure B.1).

The first series in the left panel shows the raw population data for Lakes State by single age group; this graph is very uneven across ages as discussed in chapter 1. The right panel is based on the same data but aggregated into the following age groups, 2–4, 5–9, 10–14, 15–19, and 20–24. This graph is much smoother. The second panel also shows how a polynomial curve or function was fitted to the population data. In the case of Lakes, a polynomial function of the third order fit the data very well as reflected in the high R^2. The equation of this fitted curve is also shown in the chart; this equation is the basis of calculating the smoothed population by age shown as the second series in the left panel. This procedure was repeated for all 25 states of Sudan, each time fitting a polynomial curve, although at times only a second-order polynomial function to get the best possible fit.

Tables B.1 and B.2 provide the resulting smoothed population data for South Sudan.

Figure B.1 Population by Age in Lakes State, Raw Data and Smoothed Population, 2008

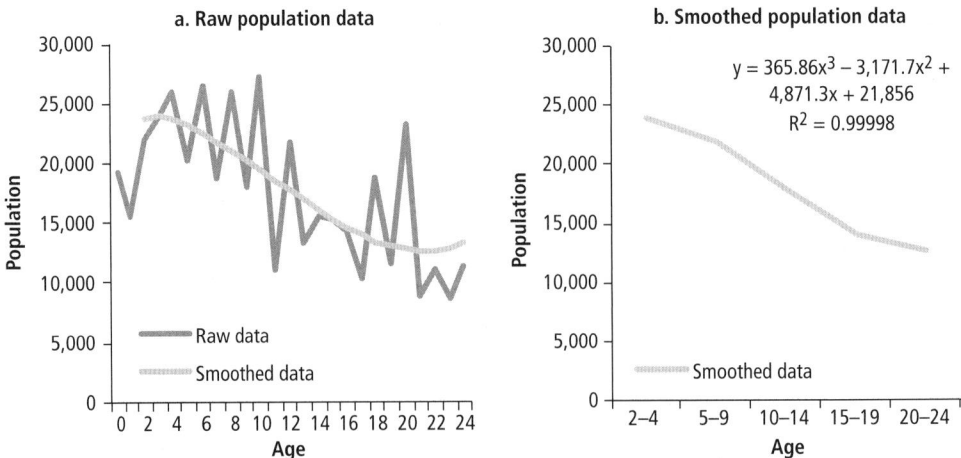

$$y = 365.86x^3 - 3,171.7x^2 + 4,871.3x + 21,856$$
$$R^2 = 0.99998$$

Source: Analysis of 2008 Population Census data.

Table B.1 Estimated Population Figures for the Republic of South Sudan, 2000–09 (based on 2008 census population)

Age	2000	2001	2002	2003	2004	2005	2006	2007	2008	2009
6	222,045	228,105	233,905	239,334	244,285	250,656	256,405	261,437	267,662	272,690
7	212,681	218,775	224,727	230,422	235,748	240,603	246,865	252,514	257,458	263,573
8	203,771	209,786	215,780	221,634	227,230	232,461	237,226	243,388	248,946	253,808
9	195,591	201,220	207,148	213,051	218,813	224,318	229,462	234,144	240,214	245,687
10	188,199	193,354	198,910	204,757	210,578	216,255	221,677	226,740	231,346	237,331
11	180,063	184,613	189,670	195,120	200,856	206,567	212,137	217,457	222,425	226,946
12	172,961	176,813	181,280	186,245	191,597	197,230	202,838	208,309	213,535	218,415
13	166,955	170,013	173,798	178,188	183,068	188,329	193,867	199,380	204,759	209,897
All ages ('000)	6,763	6,941	7,121	7,304	7,490	7,679	7,870	8,064	8,260	8,460

Source: World Bank estimation based on the 2008 Population Census.

Table B.2 Estimated Primary School-Age Population by State in the Republic of South Sudan, 2009 (based on 2008 census population)

Age	Central Equatoria	Eastern Equatoria	Western Equatoria	Jonglei	Unity	Upper Nile	Lakes	Warrap	Western Bahr Ghazal	Northern Bahr Ghazal
6	33,254	28,018	16,840	45,317	21,940	31,914	22,774	34,866	10,542	27,225
7	32,419	27,997	16,572	44,058	20,731	30,987	22,177	32,945	10,112	25,575
8	31,570	27,924	16,297	42,619	19,523	29,964	21,425	31,025	9,647	23,815
9	30,889	27,820	16,075	41,369	18,569	29,095	20,739	29,508	9,261	22,363
10	30,203	27,660	15,848	40,043	17,628	28,184	19,991	28,014	8,867	20,892
11	29,179	27,120	15,407	38,103	16,650	26,847	19,075	26,539	8,532	19,494
12	28,500	26,821	15,172	36,698	15,760	25,890	18,263	25,121	8,141	18,049
13	27,825	26,436	14,931	35,269	14,904	24,916	17,441	23,756	7,764	16,656
6–13	243,840	219,795	127,144	323,476	145,706	227,796	161,885	231,773	72,865	174,068

Source: World Bank estimation based on the 2008 Population Census.

APPENDIX C: COMPARISON OF ENROLLMENT DATA FROM DIFFERENT SOURCES

TREND IN STUDENT ENROLLMENTS BETWEEN 2000 AND 2004

There are no official, definitive data on school enrollments for the years before the Comprehensive Peace Agreement (CPA). Table C.1 presents enrollment data from various sources for an overview of available data on enrollments during the last five years before the signing of the CPA.

PRIMARY EDUCATION

Around the early 2000s, the United Nations Children's Fund (UNICEF) supported the organization of two School Baseline Assessments (SBAs) that surveyed primary schools in areas of the Republic of South Sudan controlled by the Sudan People's Liberation Movement/Army (SPLM/A).[1] The first SBA was conducted in 1999–2001 and the second in late 2002. The two SBAs found that primary school enrollments grew slightly from an estimated 331,000 around 2000 to about 343,000 at the end of 2002. By 2003–04, UNICEF estimated that primary school enrollments had grown to about 400,000.

During this time, the Federal Ministry of General Education in Khartoum also published data on school enrollments in the southern states of Sudan. According to their yearbooks, primary school enrollments in the three regions that make up South Sudan—Bahr El Ghazal, Equatoria, and Upper Nile—grew from 137,330 in 2000 to about 200,000 in 2003, to almost 400,000 in 2004, and more than 500,000 in 2005.

SECONDARY EDUCATION

According to the Federal Ministry of General Education yearbooks, enrollment in South Sudan's secondary schools was 17,465 in 2004. However, the 2006 Sudan Household Health Survey (SHHS) indicated that as many as 60,000 were attending secondary school in 2004.[2] As discussed later in chapter 2, administrative data and household data still give widely different enrollment estimates for secondary schools today.

HIGHER EDUCATION

For this level, data from the Federal Ministry for Higher Education and Scientific Research state a total enrollment of 15,102 in public universities

Table C.1   Sample Schools for the Service Delivery Study

Source	2000	2001	2002	2003	2004
Primary education:					
1. UNICEF SBA[a]	**331,000**	—	**343,000**	~400,000	—
2. SHHS[b]	—	—	—	—	~505,000
3. Khartoum Yearbooks[c]	137,330	135,782	169,167	201,467	394,356
Secondary education:					
1. SHHS[b]	—	—	—	—	~60,000
2. Khartoum Yearbooks[c]	7,740	8,163	10,215	11,951	17,465
Vocational training[c]	724	616	826	—	—
Higher education[c]	—	—	15,102	—	—

Sources: a. UNICEF School-Based Assessments conducted in 1999–2000 and end of 2002 as quoted by UNICEF (2004). The SBA covered southern Sudan SPLM/A-controlled areas only. b. Sudan Household Health Survey published in 2006, which collected data on enrollments in 2004 and 2005. c. Data collected in Khartoum (Federal Ministry of General Education or Federal Ministry of Higher Education and Scientific Research).
Note: When several sources are shown, **bold font** indicates preferred estimate.
— Not available.

in South Sudan in 2002 (1,444 at University of Bahr El Ghazal, 11,785 at Juba University, and 1,873 at Upper Nile University).

TREND IN STUDENT ENROLLMENTS BETWEEN 2005 AND 2009

Table C.2 presents data on enrollments between 2005 and 2009. For primary school enrollments, data from several different sources are shown, including EMIS and various household surveys. Data from different sources are largely consistent for primary education.

Data from different sources on secondary school enrollments are not consistent. EMIS records secondary school enrollments at 44,027 in 2009, only the second year that such data were collected by school census. These data are inconsistent with data from household surveys: around 150,000 in secondary school based on the 2009 National Baseline Household survey (and 250,000 in secondary school according to the 2008 Long Form Questionnaire). Clearly, data on secondary education are inconsistent, which is a problem that will likely be resolved over time as the data system matures and the school system stabilizes. A part of the inconsistency may be linked to youth who study abroad. In this report, the EMIS data for secondary school enrollments are used, although these may underestimate the actual secondary school population.

Table C.2   Data on Student Enrollments in the Republic of South Sudan, 2005–09

Source	2005	2006	2007	2008	2009
Primary education:					
1. RALS and EMIS[a]	—	**784,600**	**1,127,963**	**1,284,252**	**1,380,580**
2. SHHS or NBHS[b]	**~669,000**	—	—	—	1,405,316
3. Long-form questionnaire[c]	—	—	—	1,534,247	—
4. Khartoum Yearbooks[d]	519,442	—	—	—	—
Secondary education:					
1. EMIS[a]	—	—	—	25,144	44,027
2. SHHS or NBHS[b]	~61,000	—	—	—	~150,000
3. Long-form questionnaire[c]	—	—	—	248,709	—
4. Khartoum Yearbooks[d]	17,465	—	—	—	—
Higher education[a]	—	—	—	—	23,968
Teacher training[a]	—	—	—	1,259	2,445
Vocational training[a]	—	—	—	2,594	2,760
AES[a]	—	—	—	90,221	217,239

Sources: a. MoE-EMIS (2010). b. Sudan Household Health Survey (SHHS) published in 2006, which collected data on enrollments in 2004 and 2005, and National Baseline Household Survey (NBHS) that collected data for 2009. c. Long-form questionnaire of the 2008 Population Census. d. Data collected in Khartoum (Federal Ministry of General Education or Federal Ministry of Higher Education and Scientific Research).
Note: When several sources are shown, **bold font** indicates preferred estimate. — = not available. EMIS = Education Management Information Systems; RALS = Rapid Assessment of Learning Spaces.

NOTES

1. UNICEF (2004).
2. The SHHS published in 2006 asked for children's enrollment status during two consecutive years, 2004 and 2005.

APPENDIX D: METHODOLOGY FOR CALCULATION OF INDICATORS OF STUDENT FLOW

CALCULATION OF THE SCHOOLING PROFILE FOR PRIMARY AND SECONDARY EDUCATION

Figure D.1 shows two cross-sectional schooling profiles, one based on EMIS and another based on household survey data.[1] The schooling profile is not a measure of one cohort's flow through the system. Instead, it is simply a picture of the extent of access to different parts of the school system at a single point in time.

The schooling profile for the Republic of South Sudan shows a system in rapid expansion. Both schooling profiles show that access to the early grades of primary school is far larger than access to upper parts of the system. Rapid expansion of coverage and dropout explain this pattern. There are considerable differences between the two schooling profiles, however: EMIS finds much higher access to the early grades of primary than the household survey does, but lower rates of access to grade 5 onwards than the household survey.[2] These differences translate into large differences between the gross intake rate (GIR) and the primary completion rate (PCR), as can be seen in figure D.1 and table D.1.

Table D.1 compares the gross intake and primary completion rates corresponding to the two schooling profiles shown above. Given the wide

Figure D.1 Cross-Sectional Schooling Profiles Based on EMIS and NBHS, 2009

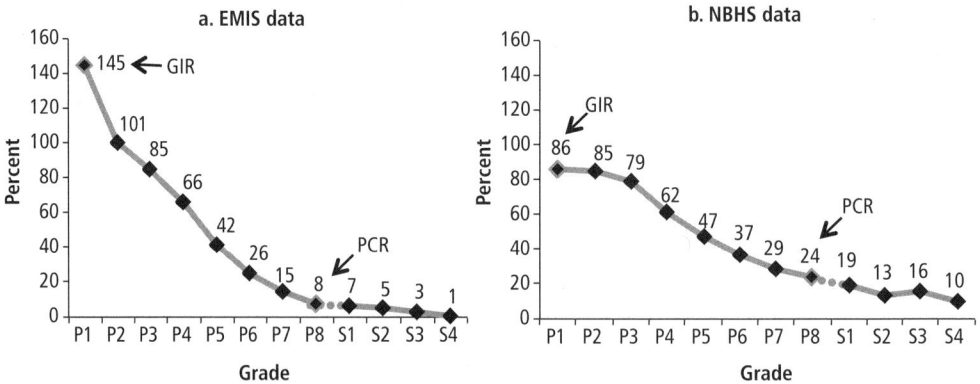

Source: Analyses of EMIS 2009 and NBHS 2009.
Note: The data points of the schooling profiles are calculated as nonrepeaters divided by population of relevant age.
PCR = primary completion rate; GIR = gross intake rate.

Table D.1   Gross Intake and Completion Rates, Primary Education, 2009

Rate	EMIS	NBHS
Gross intake rate	145%	86%
Primary completion rate, grade 6	26%	37%
Primary completion rate, grade 8	8%	24%

Source: Analysis of EMIS 2009 and NBHS 2009.

differences in the schooling profiles (and repetition structures), it is not obvious which set of intake and completion rates are more reliable. With its higher primary completion rate of 24 percent, the NBHS seems to overestimate attainment of the primary cycle, considering that only 13 percent of primary schools even offer grade 8 (as discussed in chapter 2). This suggests that the rates based on EMIS are more appropriate, although the EMIS gross intake rate does seem very high at 145 percent.

The estimates of intake and completion rates can be improved by combining EMIS and NBHS. Figure D.2 presents an adjusted schooling profile that is based on EMIS enrollment data but with the repetition structure of NBHS. As shown, the adjusted profile suggests a much lower GIR of 124 percent (instead of 145 percent) but a similar primary completion rate (7 percent instead of 8 percent).

Figure D.2   Adjusted Cross-Sectional Schooling Profile Based on EMIS, with the Repetition Structure of NBHS, 2009

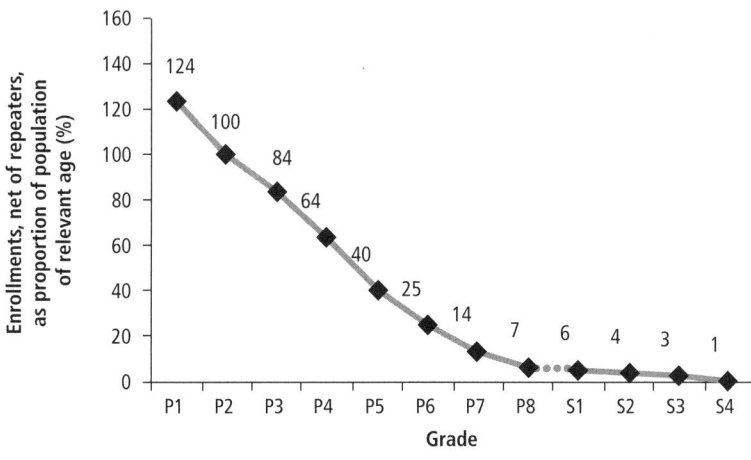

Source: Combination of data from EMIS 2009 and NBHS 2009.

CALCULATION OF RETENTION RATES FOR PRIMARY EDUCATION

Roughly one-third of students are retained until the end of the primary cycle based on reconciling the following two methods of calculation:

- The pseudo-longitudinal retention rate based on two years of EMIS data is 18 percent (table D.2). This means that 18 percent of those enrolled in grade 1 are still in school by grade 8. This rate is calculated as the product of all the promotion rates that can be observed by comparing the enrollment of nonrepeaters in one grade with the enrollment of nonrepeaters in the next grade the following year (details are shown in table D.2).
- The retention rate based on the household survey is 43 percent. This is calculated as the share of respondents who reported ever having been in school, who also say they were still in school by grade 8.

CALCULATION OF PRIMARY SCHOOL GER BY STATE

The primary school gross enrollment rate (GER[3]) was calculated based on two different data sources, (a) EMIS enrollment data combined with data

Table D.2 Promotion Rates and Retention Profile Based on Two Years of EMIS Data (pseudo-longitudinal)

Grade	Nonrepeaters 2008	Nonrepeaters 2009	Promotion rate 2008–09 (%)	Retention profile, (pseudo-longitudinal) (%)
P1	362,612	396,153	—	100
P2	219,230	265,848	73	73
P3	169,987	216,699	99	72
P4	127,038	163,317	96	70
P5	77,119	98,878	78	54
P6	46,718	58,228	76	41
P7	25,215	31,796	68	28
P8	13,038	16,192	64	18
S1	9,437	13,467	103	100
S2	6,829	9,275	98	98
S3	5,356	6,291	92	91
S4[a]	865	1,157	—	—

Source: Analysis of EMIS 2008 and 2009 combined with population data.
Note: a. The table does not provide the promotion rate between S3 and S4, because many students attend a three-year secondary school.
— Not applicable.

Figure D.3 Comparison of the Primary School GER across States Based on Two Sources, 2009

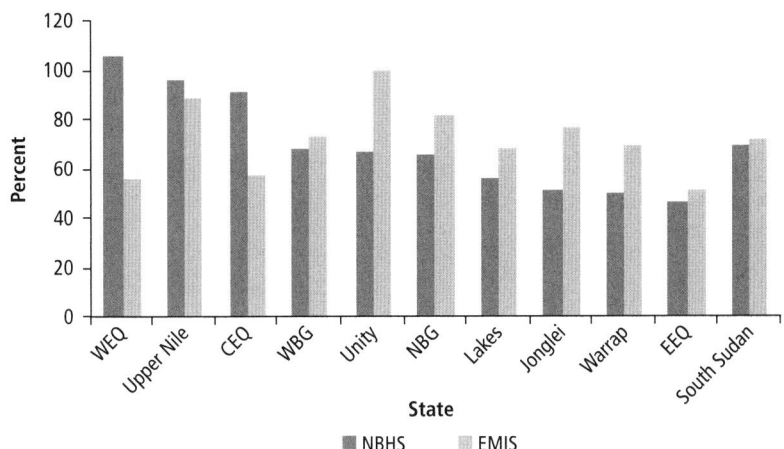

Source: Analysis of EMIS 2009 combined with population data, and NBHS 2009.

on school-age population, and (b) the NBHS. Both are shown in figure D.3. For South Sudan as a whole, the two sources produce a similar GER: 72 percent based on EMIS and 69 percent based on the NBHS. But across states, the GERs are not consistent based on the two data sources, at least not for about half the states. Of the two sources, the GER resulting from the household survey data are mostly consistent with our prior knowledge about the states, based on literacy rates and other indicators, and the NBHS is therefore chosen as the primary source for analyzing regional disparities in this report.[4]

NOTES

1. Each data point in the schooling profile corresponds to an "access rate" to that grade, which is calculated as the nonrepeaters in the grade (that is, enrollments net of repeaters) divided by the population of relevant age for the grade. The first data point is equivalent to the primary gross intake rate (GIR), while the P8 data point is equivalent to the primary completion rate (PCR).

2. Several different factors can contribute to the differences between the two schooling profiles, including flaws in age structure of the population data used for the EMIS schooling profile or sample issues in the household survey.

3. Reminder: the GER is calculated as total enrollments divided by the population of relevant age for the cycle, that is, 6–13 for primary education.

4. Perhaps the reason for the inconsistency is that the household survey rates are based on a single data source, while the rate based on EMIS and population data combines two data sources and is therefore subject to a greater margin of error.

APPENDIX E: DECOMPOSITION OF RECURRENT EDUCATION SPENDING IN THE STATES

Table E.1   Preprimary: Number of Staff on Payroll and Average Salary, 2009

State	Number of staff on payroll	Annual salary per staff on payroll	Total wage bill
Central Equatoria	172	2,203	378,964
Eastern Equatoria	239	3,250	776,832

Source: Estimation based on analysis of the payroll database.

Table E.2   Primary: Decomposition of Recurrent Spending by State and by Level of Education, 2009

State	Salary	Operating	Total
Central Equatoria	20.5	5.5	26.0
Eastern Equatoria	12.7	3.4	16.2
Jonglei	10.4	2.8	13.2
Lakes	9.7	2.6	12.3
Northern Bahr Ghazal	12.9	3.5	16.4
Unity	13.5	3.6	17.1
Upper Nile	6.7	1.8	8.5
Warrap	14.5	3.9	18.4
Western Bahr Ghazal	9.0	2.4	11.4
Western Equatoria	11.5	3.1	14.6
Total	121.5	32.7	154.2

Source: Estimation based on analysis of the payroll database.
Note: Figures include MoE's central budget broken down and distributed across levels of education and states.

Table E.3   Secondary: Decomposition of Recurrent Spending by State and by Level of Education, 2009

State	Salary	Operating	Total
National secondary	2.7	0.7	3.4
Central Equatoria	n.a.	n.a.	n.a.
Eastern Equatoria	4.6	1.2	5.9
Jonglei	3.6	1.0	4.6
Lakes	0.7	0.2	0.9
Northern Bahr Ghazal	2.5	0.7	3.1
Unity	1.9	0.5	2.5
Upper Nile	7.5	2.0	9.5
Warrap	3.2	0.8	4.0
Western Bahr Ghazal	2.6	0.7	3.3
Western Equatoria	3.8	1.0	4.8
Total	33.0	8.9	41.8

Source: Estimation based on analysis of the payroll database.
Note: Figures include MoE's central budget broken down and distributed across levels of education and states.
n.a. = Not available.

Table E.4   Alternative Education System: Decomposition of Recurrent Spending by State and by Level of Education, 2009

State	Salary	Operating	Total
Mobile teachers	2.9	0.8	3.6
Central Equatoria	n.a.	n.a.	n.a.
Eastern Equatoria	1.1	0.3	1.3
Jonglei	0.6	0.2	0.8
Lakes	0.9	0.3	1.2
Northern Bahr Ghazal	3.2	0.9	4.1
Unity	2.8	0.8	3.6
Upper Nile	1.0	0.3	1.3
Warrap	0.4	0.1	0.5
Western Bahr Ghazal	0.5	0.1	0.7
Western Equatoria	0.3	0.1	0.4
Total	13.8	3.7	17.6

Source: Estimation based on analysis of the payroll database.
Note: Figures include MoE's central budget broken down and distributed across levels of education and states.
n.a. = Not available.

APPENDIX F: EDUCATIONAL PROFILE BY STATE

Central Equatoria (1)

	CEQ	S. Sudan	Relative to S. Sudan
Demographic pressure (population age 5-16 as % of total population)	32%	33%	0.97
Literacy rate for the 15-40 age group	48%	32%	1.53
Under-5 mortality rate (poverty indicator)	141	130	1.08
"Effort": Spending per school-age child (SDG)	102	80	1.28

Enrollments and educational coverage

	Enrollments	Gross Enrollment Rate			Share of girls in total enrollments (%)		
		CEQ	S. Sudan	Relative to S. Sudan	CEQ	S. Sudan	Relative to S. Sudan
Primary education	231,066	91%	69%	1.33	46%	37%	1.24
Secondary education	42,200	39%	20%	1.89	35%	27%	1.29
AES[1]	25,156	11%	9%	1.15	40%	42%	0.95

[1] Enrollment/Non-literate population in the 15-40 age group

Student annual growth rate 2006 to 2009

	CEQ	S. Sudan
Primary education	13%	25%

Central Equatoria (2)

Cohort rates   Gross rates

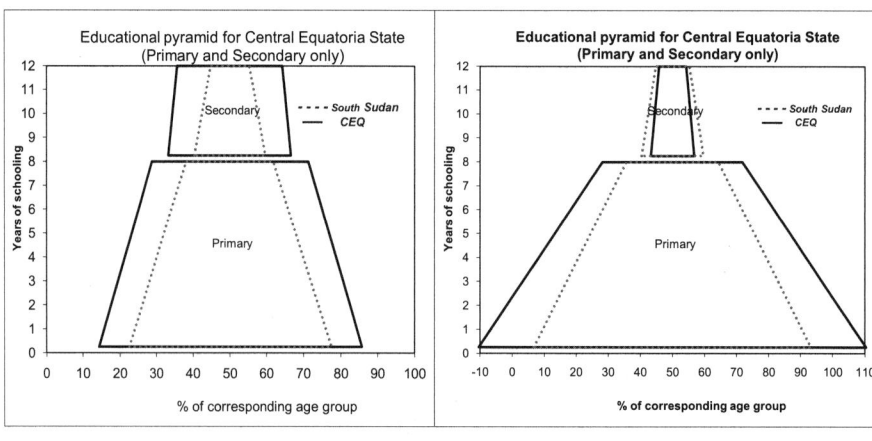

Central Equatoria (3)

Government school: Teachers and other staff

	Pupil teacher ratio		Volunteers as % of all school-based staff		Non-school based staff as % of all staff	
	CEQ	S. Sudan	CEQ	S. Sudan	CEQ	S. Sudan
Primary education	32	52	17%	48%	17%	20%

Government school: Facilities

	Students Per School			Pupils Per Classroom		
	CEQ	S. Sudan	Relative to S. Sudan	CEQ	S. Sudan	Relative to S. Sudan
Primary education	322	429	0.75	77	129	0.59

Per Student Spending at State Level

	Central Equatoria			Relative to South Sudan		
SDG	Primary	Secondary	AES	Primary	Secondary	AES
Total	136	217	64	1.2	0.6	0.7
Salary	107	171	51			
Operating	29	46	14			

Central Equatoria (4)

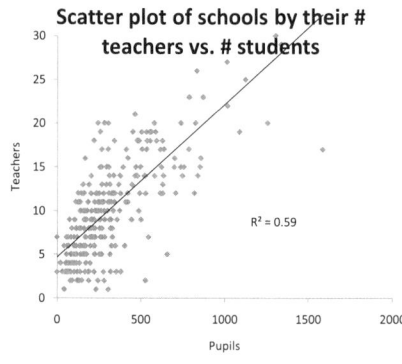

Scatter plot of schools by their # teachers vs. # students

$R^2 = 0.59$

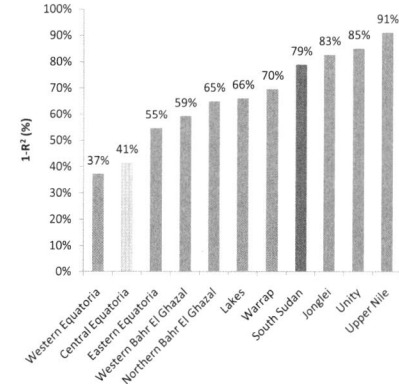

Eastern Equatoria (1)

	EEQ	S. Sudan	Relative to S. Sudan
Demographic pressure (population age 5-16 as % of total population)	36%	33%	1.08
Literacy rate for the 15-40 age group	21%	32%	0.67
Under-5 mortality rate (poverty indicator)	118	130	0.91
"Effort": Spending per school-age child (SDG)	76	80	0.95

Enrollments and educational coverage

	Enrollments	Gross Enrollment Rate			Share of girls in total enrollments (%)		
		EEQ	S. Sudan	Relative to S. Sudan	EEQ	S. Sudan	Relative to S. Sudan
Primary education	102,182	46%	69%	0.67	40%	37%	1.08
Secondary education	11,312	13%	20%	0.66	25%	27%	0.91
AES[1]	15,440	5%	9%	0.56	37%	42%	0.87

[1] Enrollment/Non-literate population in the 15-40 age group

Student annual growth rate 2006 to 2009

	EEQ	S. Sudan
Primary education	30%	25%

Eastern Equatoria (2)

Cohort rates   ## Gross rates

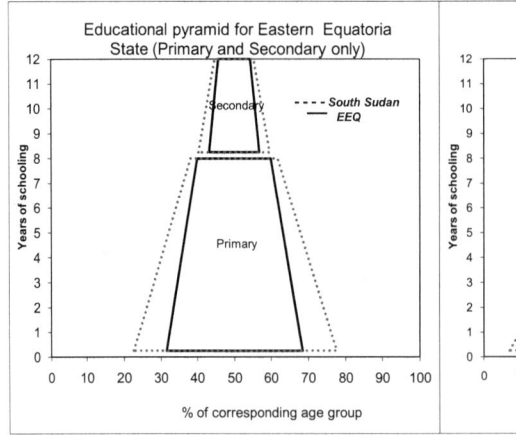

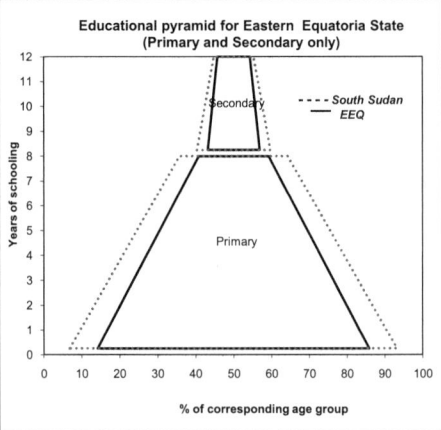

Eastern Equatoria (3)

Government school: Teachers and other staff

	Pupil teacher ratio		Volunteers as % of all school-based staff		Non-school based staff as % of all staff	
	EEQ	S. Sudan	EEQ	S. Sudan	EEQ	S. Sudan
Primary education	38	52	16%	48%	13%	20%

Government school: Facilities

	Students Per School			Pupils Per Classroom		
	EEQ	S. Sudan	Relative to S. Sudan	EEQ	S. Sudan	Relative to S. Sudan
Primary education	382	429	0.89	131	129	1.01

Per Student Spending at State Level

	Eastern Equatoria			Relative to South Sudan		
SDG	Primary	Secondary	AES	Primary	Secondary	AES
Total	165	524	87	1.4	1.5	1.0
Salary	130	413	69			
Operating	35	111	18			

Eastern Equatoria (4)

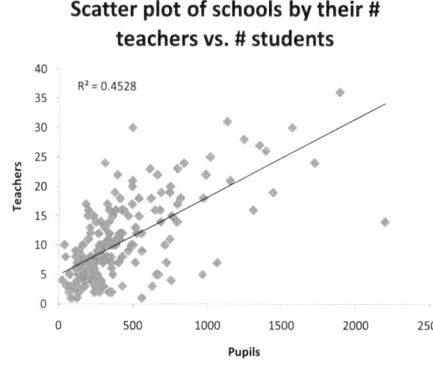

Scatter plot of schools by their # teachers vs. # students

R² = 0.4528

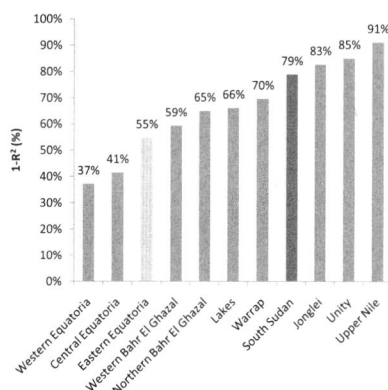

Jonglei (1)

	Jonglei	S. Sudan	Relative to S. Sudan
Demographic pressure (population age 5-16 as % of total population)	34%	33%	1.02
Literacy rate for the 15-40 age group	20%	32%	0.62
Under-5 mortality rate (poverty indicator)	108	130	0.83
"Effort": Spending per school-age child (SDG)	41	80	0.51

Enrollments and educational coverage

	Enrollments	Gross Enrollment Rate			Share of girls in total enrollments (%)		
		Jonglei	S. Sudan	Relative to S. Sudan	Jonglei	S. Sudan	Relative to S. Sudan
Primary education	155,676	51%	69%	0.74	38%	37%	1.03
Secondary education	6,824	6%	20%	0.31	26%	27%	0.93
AES[1]	33,085	7%	9%	0.79	45%	42%	1.06

[1] Enrollment/Non-literate population in the 15-40 age group

Student annual growth rate 2006 to 2009

	Jonglei	S. Sudan
Primary education	32%	25%

Jonglei (2)

Cohort rates

Gross rates

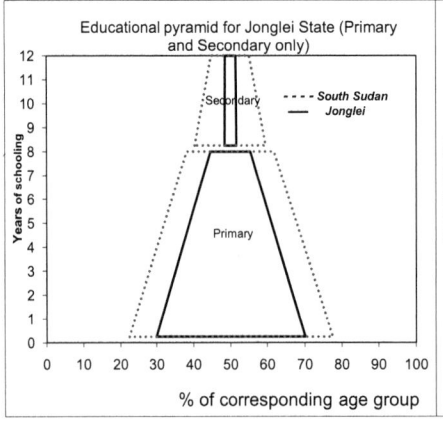

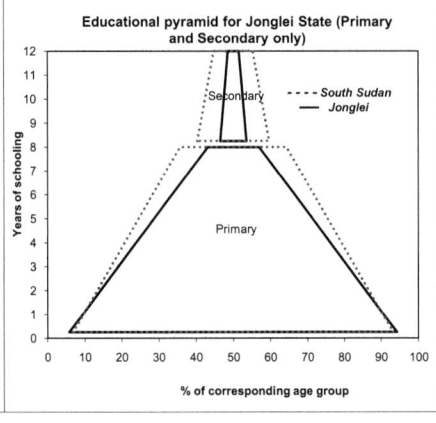

Jonglei (3)

Government school: Teachers and other staff

	Pupil teacher ratio		Volunteers as % of all school-based staff		Non-school based staff as % of all staff	
	Jonglei	S. Sudan	*Jonglei*	S. Sudan	*Jonglei*	S. Sudan
Primary education	84	52	68%	48%	20%	20%

Government school: Facilities

	Students Per School			Pupils Per Classroom		
	Jonglei	S. Sudan	Relative to S. Sudan	Jonglei	S. Sudan	Relative to S. Sudan
Primary education	607	429	1.42	169	129	1.30

Per Student Spending at State Level

SDG	Jonglei			Relative to South Sudan		
	Primary	Secondary	AES	Primary	Secondary	AES
Total	**87**	**734**	**24**	0.7	2.1	0.3
Salary	69	578	19			
Operating	18	156	5			

Jonglei (4)

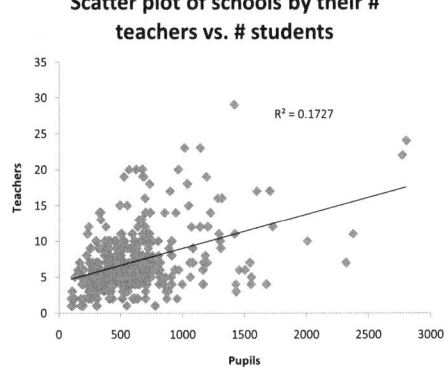

Scatter plot of schools by their # teachers vs. # students

$R^2 = 0.1727$

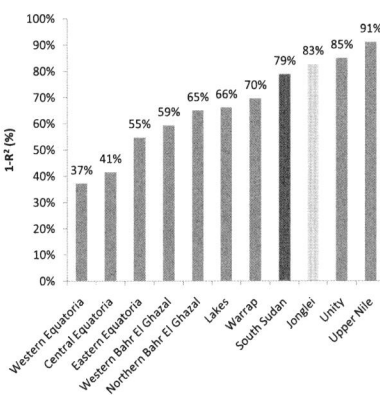

Lakes (1)

	Lakes	S. Sudan	Relative to S. Sudan
Demographic pressure (population age 5-16 as % of total population)	33%	33%	0.99
Literacy rate for the 15-40 age group	21%	32%	0.66
Under-5 mortality rate (poverty indicator)	114	130	0.88
"Effort": Spending per school-age child (SDG)	63	80	0.79

Enrollments and educational coverage

	Enrollments	Gross Enrollment Rate			Share of girls in total enrollments (%)		
		Lakes	S. Sudan	Relative to S. Sudan	Lakes	S. Sudan	Relative to S. Sudan
Primary education	94,145	56%	69%	0.81	31%	37%	0.84
Secondary education	10,230	17%	20%	0.83	6%	27%	0.21
AES[1]	17,624	8%	9%	0.83	45%	42%	1.05

[1] Enrollment/Non-literate population in the 15-40 age group

Student annual growth rate 2006 to 2009

	Lakes	S. Sudan
Primary education	10%	25%

Lakes (2)

Cohort rates   ## Gross rates

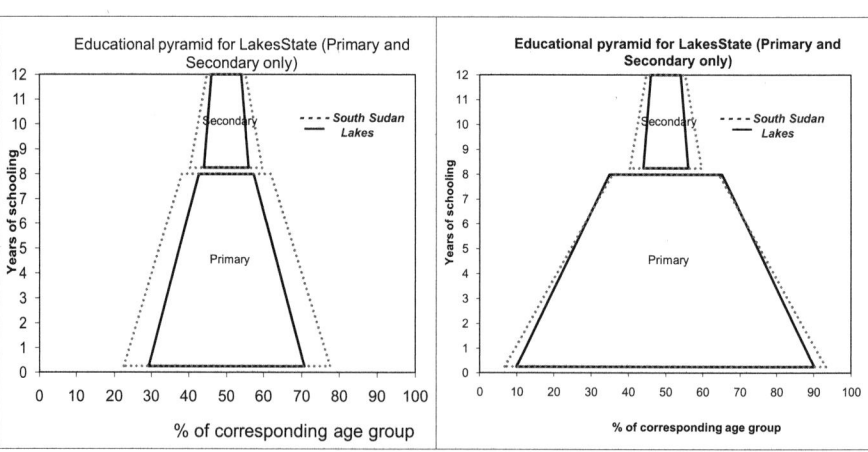

Lakes (3)

Government school: Teachers and other staff

	Pupil teacher ratio		Volunteers as % of all school-based staff		Non-school based staff as % of all staff	
	Lakes	S. Sudan	Lakes	S. Sudan	Lakes	S. Sudan
Primary education	50	52	56%	48%	17%	20%

Government school: Facilities

	Students Per School			Pupils Per Classroom		
	Lakes	S. Sudan	Relative to S. Sudan	Lakes	S. Sudan	Relative to S. Sudan
Primary education	395	429	0.92	138	129	1.07

Per Student Spending at State Level

	Lakes			Relative to South Sudan		
SDG	Primary	Secondary	AES	Primary	Secondary	AES
Total	**134**	**98**	**68**	1.1	0.3	0.8
Salary	106	77	54			
Operating	29	21	15			

Lakes (4)

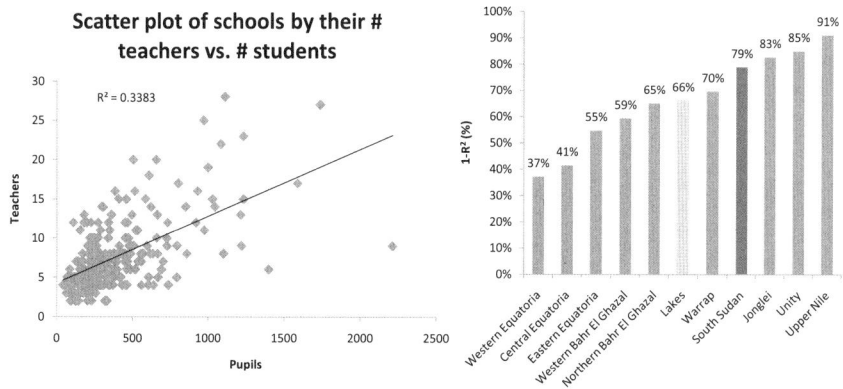

Northern Bahr El Ghazal (1)

	NBG	S. Sudan	Relative to S. Sudan
Demographic pressure (population age 5-16 as % of total population)	32%	33%	0.98
Literacy rate for the 15-40 age group	28%	32%	0.89
Under-5 mortality rate (poverty indicator)	165	130	1.27
"Effort": Spending per school-age child (SDG)	101	80	1.26

Enrollments and educational coverage

	Enrollments	Gross Enrollment Rate			Share of girls in total enrollments (%)		
		NBG	S. Sudan	Relative to S. Sudan	NBG	S. Sudan	Relative to S. Sudan
Primary education	126,955	65%	69%	0.95	32%	37%	0.86
Secondary education	9,959	15%	20%	0.75	9%	27%	0.32
AES[1]	39,313	18%	9%	1.97	33%	42%	0.79

[1] Enrollment/Non-literate population in the 15-40 age group

Student annual growth rate 2006 to 2009

	NBG	S. Sudan
Primary education	25%	25%

Northern Bahr El Ghazal (2)

Cohort rates

Gross rates

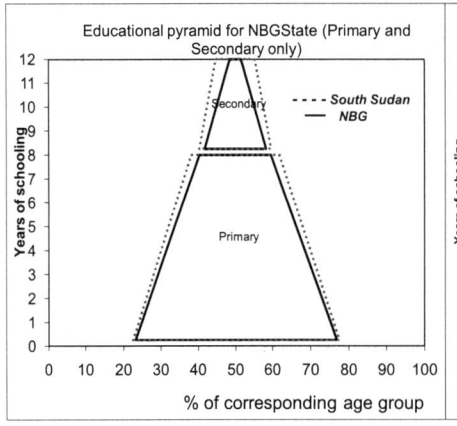

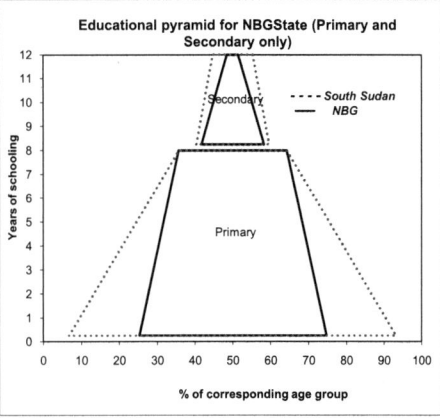

Northern Bahr El Ghazal (3)

Government school: Teachers and other staff

	Pupil teacher ratio		Volunteers as % of all school-based staff		Non-school based staff as % of all staff	
	NBG	S. Sudan	NBG	S. Sudan	NBG	S. Sudan
Primary education	56	52	64%	48%	21%	20%

Government school: Facilities

	Students Per School			Pupils Per Classroom		
	NBG	S. Sudan	Relative to S. Sudan	NBG	S. Sudan	Relative to S. Sudan
Primary education	429	429	1.00	140	129	1.08

Per Student Spending at State Level

	NBG			Relative to South Sudan		
SDG	Primary	Secondary	AES	Primary	Secondary	AES
Total	**132**	**330**	**103**	1.1	0.9	1.2
Salary	104	260	81			
Operating	28	70	22			

Northern Bahr El Ghazal (4)

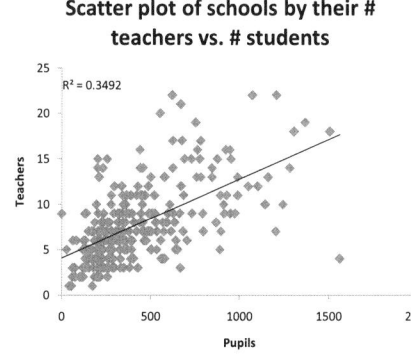

Scatter plot of schools by their # teachers vs. # students

$R^2 = 0.3492$

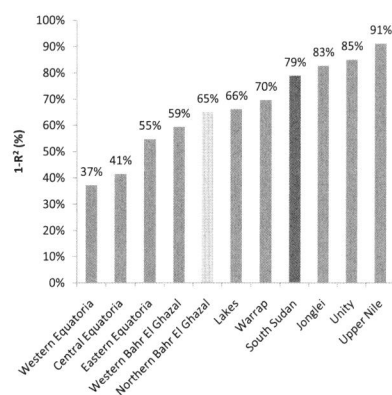

Unity (1)

	Unity	S. Sudan	Relative to S. Sudan
Demographic pressure (population age 5-16 as % of total population)	34%	33%	1.04
Literacy rate for the 15-40 age group	32%	32%	1.02
Under-5 mortality rate (poverty indicator)	82	130	0.63
"Effort": Spending per school-age child (SDG)	115	80	1.44

Enrollments and educational coverage

	Enrollments	Gross Enrollment Rate			Share of girls in total enrollments (%)		
		Unity	S. Sudan	Relative to S. Sudan	Unity	S. Sudan	Relative to S. Sudan
Primary education	88,808	67%	69%	0.98	33%	37%	0.90
Secondary education	6,096	16%	20%	0.77	9%	27%	0.35
AES[1]	40,967	25%	9%	2.68	43%	42%	1.02

[1] Enrollment/Non-literate population in the 15-40 age group

Student annual growth rate 2006 to 2009

	Unity	S. Sudan
Primary education	39%	25%

Unity (2)

Cohort rates   Gross rates

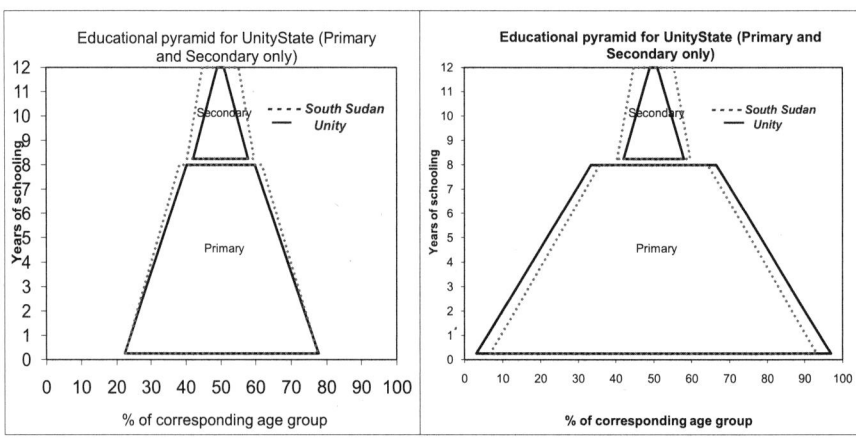

Unity (3)

Government school: Teachers and other staff

	Pupil teacher ratio		Volunteers as % of all school-based staff		Non-school based staff as % of all staff	
	Unity	S. Sudan	Unity	S. Sudan	Unity	S. Sudan
Primary education	61	52	50%	48%	12%	20%

Government school: Facilities

	Students Per School			Pupils Per Classroom		
	Unity	S. Sudan	Relative to S. Sudan	Unity	S. Sudan	Relative to S. Sudan
Primary education	508	429	1.17	182	129	1.41

Per Student Spending at State Level

	Unity			Relative to South Sudan		
SDG	Primary	Secondary	AES	Primary	Secondary	AES
Total	200	402	87	1.7	1.2	1.0
Salary	158	317	69			
Operating	42	85	18			

Unity (4)

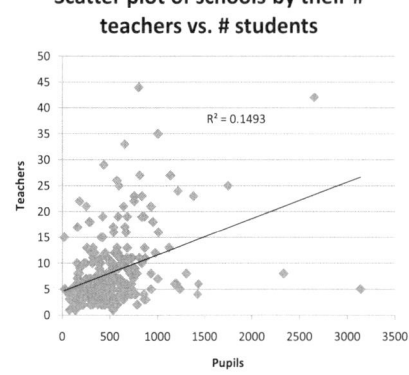

Scatter plot of schools by their # teachers vs. # students

$R^2 = 0.1493$

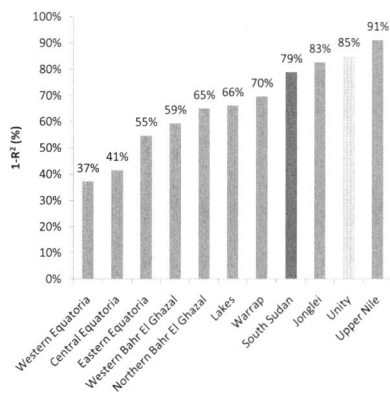

Upper Nile (1)

	UNS	S. Sudan	Relative to S. Sudan
Demographic pressure (population age 5-16 as % of total population)	33%	33%	1.01
Literacy rate for the 15-40 age group	54%	32%	1.71
Under-5 mortality rate (poverty indicator)	110	130	0.85
"Effort": Spending per school-age child (SDG)	60	80	0.75

Enrollments and educational coverage

	Enrollments	Gross Enrollment Rate			Share of girls in total enrollments (%)		
		UNS	S. Sudan	Relative to S. Sudan	UNS	S. Sudan	Relative to S. Sudan
Primary education	265,806	96%	69%	1.39	41%	37%	1.11
Secondary education	34,828	35%	20%	1.72	30%	27%	1.09
AES[1]	29,915	16%	9%	1.76	53%	42%	1.26

[1] Enrollment/Non-literate population in the 15-40 age group

Student annual growth rate 2006 to 2009

	UNS	S. Sudan
Primary education	32%	25%

Upper Nile (2)

Cohort rates　　　　　　　　　　Gross rates

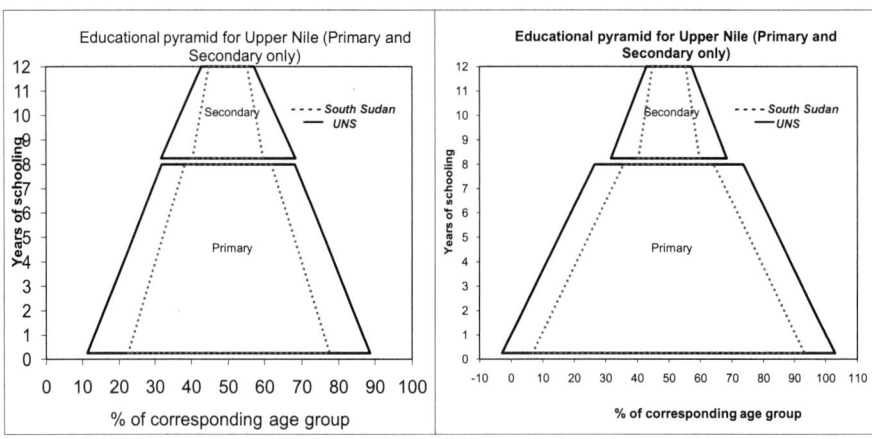

Upper Nile (3)

Government school: Teachers and other staff

	Pupil teacher ratio		Volunteers as % of all school-based staff		Non-school based staff as % of all staff	
	UNS	S. Sudan	UNS	S. Sudan	UNS	S. Sudan
Primary education	70	52	63%	48%	31%	20%

Government school: Facilities

	Students Per School			Pupils Per Classroom		
	UNS	S. Sudan	Relative to S. Sudan	UNS	S. Sudan	Relative to S. Sudan
Primary education	569	429	1.33	165	129	1.27

Per Student Spending at State Level

	UNS			Relative to South Sudan		
SDG	Primary	Secondary	AES	Primary	Secondary	AES
Total	**35**	**290**	**44**	0.3	0.8	0.5
Salary	27	228	35			
Operating	7	62	9			

Upper Nile (4)

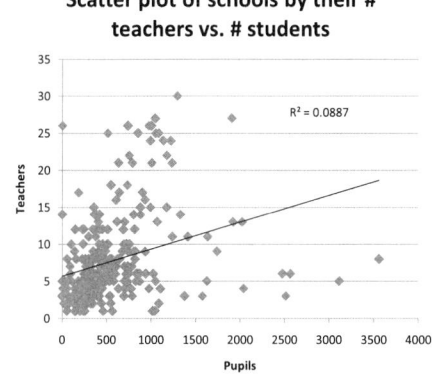

Scatter plot of schools by their # teachers vs. # students

$R^2 = 0.0887$

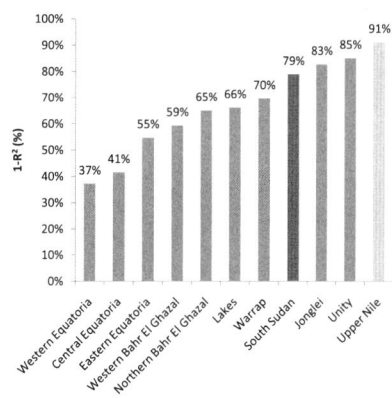

Warrap (1)

	Warrap	S. Sudan	Relative to S. Sudan
Demographic pressure (population age 5-16 as % of total population)	33%	33%	1.00
Literacy rate for the 15-40 age group	19%	32%	0.61
Under-5 mortality rate (poverty indicator)	176	130	1.35
"Effort": Spending per school-age child (SDG)	72	80	0.90

Enrollments and educational coverage

	Enrollments	Gross Enrollment Rate			Share of girls in total enrollments (%)		
		Warrap	S. Sudan	Relative to S. Sudan	Warrap	S. Sudan	Relative to S. Sudan
Primary education	130,264	50%	69%	0.72	29%	37%	0.79
Secondary education	14,480	15%	20%	0.72	10%	27%	0.38
AES[1]	5,306	2%	9%	0.18	36%	42%	0.84

[1] Enrollment/Non-literate population in the 15-40 age group

Student annual growth rate 2006 to 2009

	Warrap	S. Sudan
Primary education	22%	25%

Warrap (2)

Cohort rates

Gross rates

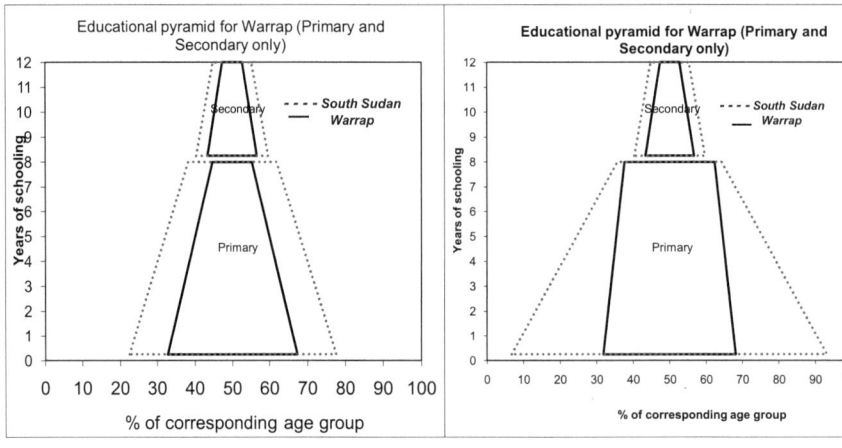

Warrap (3)

Government school: Teachers and other staff

	Pupil teacher ratio		Volunteers as % of all school-based staff		Non-school based staff as % of all staff	
	Warrap	S. Sudan	Warrap	S. Sudan	Warrap	S. Sudan
Primary education	50	52	55%	48%	19%	20%

Government school: Facilities

	Students Per School			Pupils Per Classroom		
	Warrap	S. Sudan	Relative to S. Sudan	Warrap	S. Sudan	Relative to S. Sudan
Primary education	446	429	1.04	111	129	0.86

Per Student Spending at State Level

	Warrap			Relative to South Sudan		
SDG	Primary	Secondary	AES	Primary	Secondary	AES
Total	**143**	**277**	**98**	1.7	1.2	1.0
Salary	113	219	77			
Operating	30	58	21			

Warrap (4)

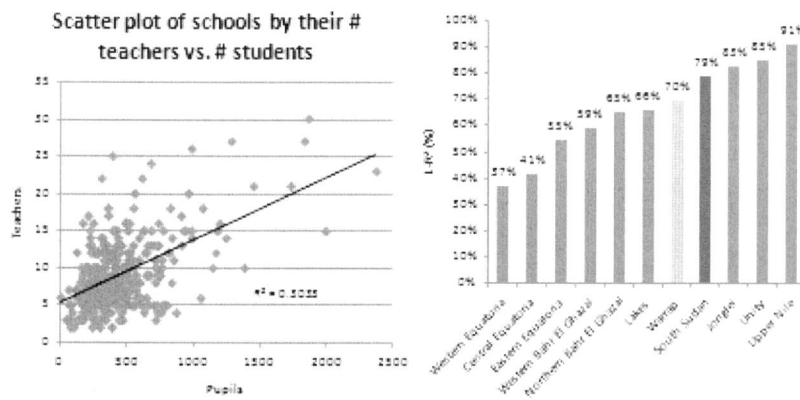

Western Bahr El Ghazal (1)

	WBG	S. Sudan	Relative to S. Sudan
Demographic pressure (population age 5-16 as % of total population)	31%	33%	0.92
Literacy rate for the 15-40 age group	39%	32%	1.22
Under-5 mortality rate (poverty indicator)	134	130	1.03
"Effort": Spending per school-age child (SDG)	152	80	1.90

Enrollments and educational coverage

	Enrollments	Gross Enrollment Rate			Share of girls in total enrollments (%)		
		WBG	S. Sudan	Relative to S. Sudan	WBG	S. Sudan	Relative to S. Sudan
Primary education	52,275	68%	69%	0.99	38%	37%	1.03
Secondary education	6,562	25%	20%	1.23	23%	27%	0.86
AES[1]	5,048	6%	9%	0.64	41%	42%	0.96

[1] Enrollment/Non-literate population in the 15-40 age group

Student annual growth rate 2006 to 2009

	WBG	S. Sudan
Primary education	22%	25%

Western Bahr El Ghazal (2)

Cohort rates   ## Gross rates

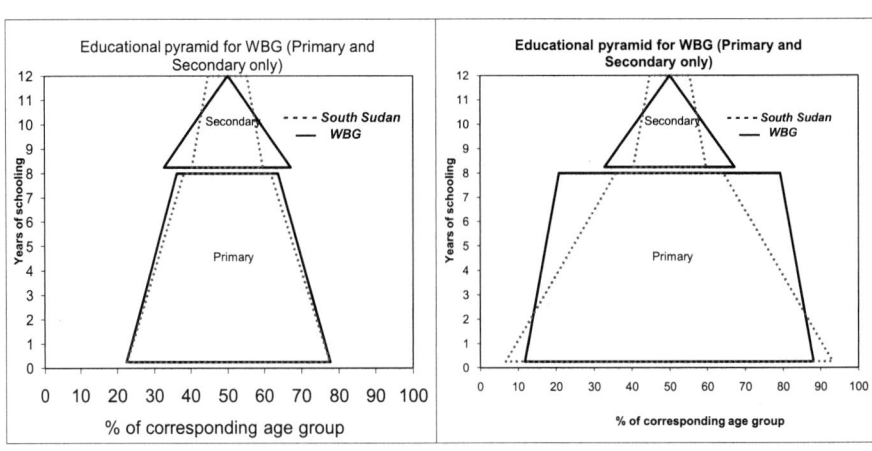

Western Bahr El Ghazal (3)

Government school: Teachers and other staff

	Pupil teacher ratio		Volunteers as % of all school-based staff		Non-school based staff as % of all staff	
	WBG	S. Sudan	WBG	S. Sudan	WBG	S. Sudan
Primary education	48	52	37%	48%	44%	20%

Government school: Facilities

	Students Per School			Pupils Per Classroom		
	WBG	S. Sudan	Relative to S. Sudan	WBG	S. Sudan	Relative to S. Sudan
Primary education	414	429	0.97	98	129	0.76

Per Student Spending at State Level

	WBG			Relative to South Sudan		
SDG	Primary	Secondary	AES	Primary	Secondary	AES
Total	259	740	133	2.2	2.1	1.5
Salary	204	583	105			
Operating	55	157	28			

Western Bahr El Ghazal (4)

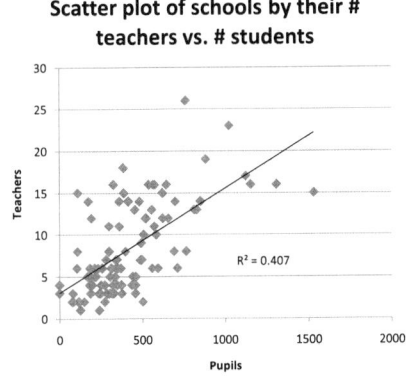

Scatter plot of schools by their # teachers vs. # students

$R^2 = 0.407$

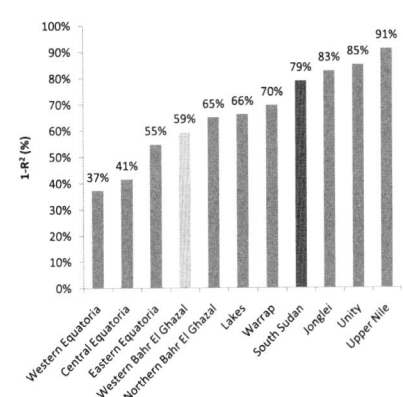

Western Equatoria (1)

	WEQ	S. Sudan	Relative to S. Sudan
Demographic pressure (population age 5-16 as % of total population)	30%	33%	0.91
Literacy rate for the 15-40 age group	37%	32%	1.15
Under-5 mortality rate (poverty indicator)	192	130	1.48
"Effort": Spending per school-age child (SDG)	106	80	1.33

Enrollments and educational coverage

	Enrollments	Gross Enrollment Rate			Share of girls in total enrollments (%)		
		WEQ	S. Sudan	Relative to S. Sudan	WEQ	S. Sudan	Relative to S. Sudan
Primary education	158,184	106%	69%	1.54	44%	37%	1.20
Secondary education	9,852	18%	20%	0.87	28%	27%	1.01
AES[1]	5,385	3%	9%	0.36	54%	42%	1.28

[1] Enrollment/Non-literate population in the 15-40 age group

Student annual growth rate 2006 to 2009

	WEQ	S. Sudan
Primary education	20%	25%

Western Equatoria (2)

Cohort rates

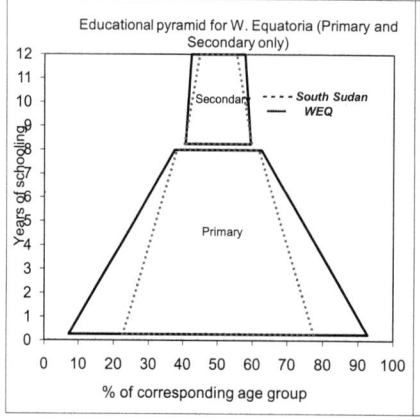

Gross rates

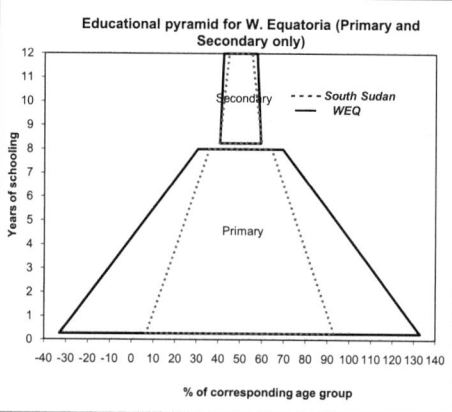

Western Equatoria (3)

Government school: Teachers and other staff

	Pupil teacher ratio		Volunteers as % of all school-based staff		Non-school based staff as % of all staff	
	WEQ	S. Sudan	WEQ	S. Sudan	WEQ	S. Sudan
Primary education	34	52	62%	48%	22%	20%

Government school: Facilities

	Students Per School			Pupils Per Classroom		
	WEQ	S. Sudan	Relative to S. Sudan	WEQ	S. Sudan	Relative to S. Sudan
Primary education	203	429	0.47	99	129	0.76

Per Student Spending at State Level

	WEQ			Relative to South Sudan		
SDG	Primary	Secondary	AES	Primary	Secondary	AES
Total	100	532	77	0.8	1.5	0.9
Salary	79	420	61			
Operating	21	112	16			

Western Equatoria (4)

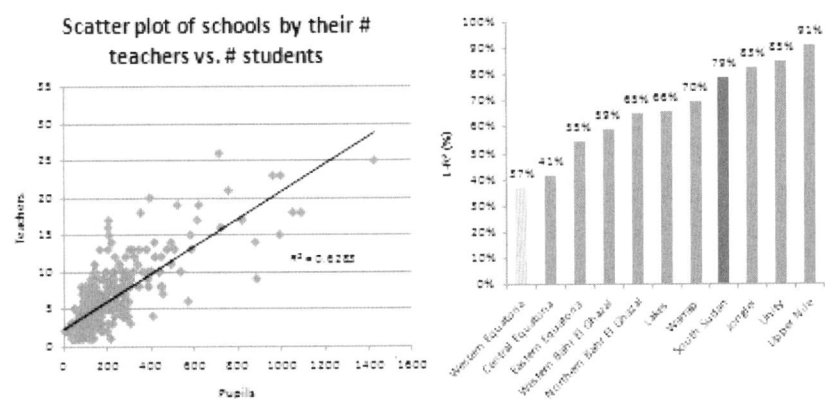

References

Avenstrup, R., X. Liang, and S. Nellemann. 2004. *Kenya, Lesotho, Malawi and Uganda: Universal Primary Education and Poverty Reduction.* Washington, DC: World Bank.

Booz & Company. 2010. "Lessons Learnt Exercise on Data Gathering and Payroll Implementation." London, UK: Booz & Company. Available at: http://www.cbtf-southsudan.org/sites/default/files/lessons_learned_exercise_on_data_gathering_and_payroll_implementation_-_revised_draft_0.pdf.

Brophy, M. 2003. "Progress to Universal Primary Education in Southern Sudan: A Short Country Case Study." Background paper prepared for the *Education for All Global Monitoring Report 2003/4: Gender and Education for All: The Leap to Equity.* Prepared for the United Nations Educational, Scientific, and Cultural Organization (UNESCO). Paris: UNESCO.

Glick, P., and D. Sahn. 2010. "Early Academic Performance, Grade Repetition, and School Attainment in Senegal." *World Bank Economic Review* 24 (1): 93–120.

Goldsmith, C. 2010. "Teachers' Pay—Making the Pipe Work: The Role of Improving Teachers' Payroll Systems for Education Service Delivery and State Legitimacy in Selected Conflict-Affected Countries in Africa." Paper commissioned for the *Education for All Global Monitoring Report 2011: The Hidden Crisis: Armed Conflict and Education.* Prepared for UNESCO. Paris: UNESCO.

Government of National Unity, Ministry of General Education (GoNU-MoGE). 2001–06. *Educational Statistics.* Yearbooks prepared by the General Directorate of Educational Planning, Ministry of Education of the then-Government of Sudan, later Government of National Unity, Khartoum.

Hjort, H. 2008. "Technical Review of the Quality of Construction of Primary Schools and County Education Centres and Assessment of Contract Management Capacity and Performance." MDTF Education, Southern Sudan, World Bank, Washington, DC.

International Association for the Evaluation of Educational Achievement (IEA). 2008. *Report from Test Administration in Benin.* Hamburg: International Association for the Evaluation of Educational Achievement.

International Organization for Migration (IOM). 2009a. "State Report Unity—Villages Assessments and Returnee Monitoring." Juba, South Sudan.

———. 2009b. "State Report Northern Bahr Ghazal—Villages Assessments and Returnee Monitoring." Juba, South Sudan.

————. 2009c. "State Report Warrap—Village Assessments and Returnee Monitoring." Juba, South Sudan.

Majgaard, K., and A. Mingat. 2012. *Education in Sub-Saharan Africa: A Comparative Analysis.* Washington, DC: World Bank.

Ministry of Education, Science and Technology (MoEST). 2007. "Fast Track Teacher Education and Training Program." Juba: MoEST (now MoE), the Republic of South Sudan.

————. 2009. "National Teacher Education Strategy." Juba: Republic of South Sudan.

Ministry of Education, Science and Technology and United Nations Children's Fund (MoEST/UNICEF). 2006. *Rapid Assessment of Learning Spaces. Southern Sudan.* New York, NY: UNICEF.

————. 2008. *Socioeconomic and Cultural Barriers to Schooling in Southern Sudan.* Final Report. New York, NY: UNICEF.

Ministry of Education, Science and Technology, Department of Alternative Education Systems (MoEST-AES). 2008a. *Pastoralist Rapid Assessment Report.* Prepared by Peter Deng Aguer, Department of Alternative Education Systems. Juba: Republic of South Sudan.

————. 2008b. *Alternative Education Systems: Implementation Guide.* Department of Alternative Education Systems. Juba: Republic of South Sudan.

MoE-AES. 2011. *Eye on Literacy. Facts, Myth, Analytical Views.* Publication of the Directorate for Alternative Education Systems.

Ministry of Education, Education Management Information System (MoE-EMIS). 2009. *Draft EMIS Education Statistics 2008.* Version 1.2, February 2009. Juba: Republic of South Sudan.

————. 2010. *Education Statistics for Southern Sudan 2009.* National Statistical Booklet. Version 2.0. Juba: Republic of South Sudan.

Ministry of Finance and Economic Planning (MoFEP). 2007. *Approved Budget 2008.* Juba: Government of the Republic of South Sudan (GoRSS).

————. 2009a. *Approved Budget 2009.* Juba: GoRSS.

————. 2009b. *Donor Book 2009.* Juba: GoRSS.

————. 2010. *Approved Budget 2010.* Juba: GoRSS.

National Baseline Household Survey (NBHS). 2009. *National Baseline Household Survey.* Household survey conducted by the Southern Sudan Centre for Census, Statistics and Evaluation (SSCCSE). Nationally representative for the Republic of South Sudan.

Pôle de Dakar 2010. Database of education performance indicators maintained and updated annually by Pole de Dakar, www.poledakar.org.

Service Delivery Study (SDS). 2010. *Service Delivery Study.* School survey conducted for the Ministry of Education by Juba University and Southern Sudan Centre for Census, Statistics and Evaluation (SSCCSE) in cooperation with the World Bank and with financial support from the Multi-Donor Trust Fund for Southern Sudan.

Southern Sudan Centre for Census, Statistics and Evaluation (SSCCSE). 2008. "Fifth Sudan Population and Housing Census 2008." Juba: GoRSS.

————. 2010a. *Statistical Yearbook for Southern Sudan 2009.* Juba: GoRSS.

————. 2010b. *Key Indicators for Southern Sudan.* Juba: GoRSS.

————. 2010c. *Poverty in Southern Sudan.* Estimates from NBHS 2009. Juba: GoRSS.

Sommers, M. 2005. *Islands of Education: Schooling, Civil War and the Southern Sudanese (1983–2004).* International Institute for Educational Planning, UNESCO. Paris: UNESCO.

Sudan Household Health Survey (SHHS). 2006. *Sudan Household Health Survey.* Household survey conducted by the Sudanese Federal Ministry of Health and the Central Bureau of Statistics of the Government of National Unity and the Ministry of Health and the Southern Sudan Commission for Census Statistics and Evaluation of the Government of Southern Sudan.

United Nations Children's Fund (UNICEF). 2004. *Towards a Baseline: Best Estimates of Social Indicators for Southern Sudan.* New Sudan Centre for Statistics and Evaluation in Association with UNICEF.

———. 2009. *Socio Economic and Cultural Barriers to Schooling in South Sudan.* New Sudan Centre for Statistics and Evaluation in Association with UNICEF.

United States Agency for International Development (USAID). 2009. *The Status of Teacher Professional Development in Southern Sudan.* Washington, DC: USAID.

World Bank. 2007. *Sudan: Public Expenditure Review.* Synthesis Report. Washington, DC: World Bank.

———. 2009. *Sudan: Toward Sustainable and Broad-Based Growth.* Country Economic Memorandum. Washington, DC: World Bank.

———. 2011a. *Sudan Poverty Assessment: Part II. Poverty Profile for Southern States.* Draft. Washington, DC: World Bank.

———. 2011b. *Sudan Poverty Assessment: Population Health Profile.* Draft. Washington, DC: World Bank.

World Bank. 2012. *The Status of the Education Sector in Sudan.* Washington, DC: World Bank.